CAMPAIGN 371

THE BATTLE OF HUE 1968

Fight for the Imperial City

JAMES H. WILLBANKS   ILLUSTRATED BY RAMIRO BUJEIRO

Series editor Nikolai Bogdanovic

OSPREY PUBLISHING
Bloomsbury Publishing Plc
PO Box 883, Oxford, OX1 9PL, UK
29 Earlsfort Terrace, Dublin 2, Ireland
1385 Broadway, 5th Floor, New York, NY 10018, USA
E-mail: info@ospreypublishing.com
www.ospreypublishing.com

OSPREY is a trademark of Osprey Publishing Ltd

First published in Great Britain in 2021

A catalog record for this book is available from the British Library.

ISBN: PB 9781472844712; eBook 9781472844651; ePDF 9781472844637; XML 9781472844644

21 22 23 24 25   10 9 8 7 6 5 4 3 2 1

Maps by Bounford.com
3D BEVs by Paul Kime
Index by Zoe Ross
Typeset by PDQ Digital Media Solutions, Bungay, UK
Printed and bound in India by Replika Press Private Ltd.

Artist's note

Readers may care to note that the original paintings from which the color plates in this book were prepared are available for private sale. All reproduction copyright whatsoever is retained by the publishers. The artist can be contacted at the following email address:

ramirobujeiro@yahoo.com.ar

The publishers regret that they can enter into no correspondence upon this matter.

Osprey Publishing supports the Woodland Trust, the UK's leading woodland conservation charity.

To find out more about our authors and books visit **www.ospreypublishing.com**. Here you will find extracts, author interviews, details of forthcoming events and the option to sign up for our newsletter.

Unit abbreviations

US company, battalion and regiment names frequently appear in abbreviated form throughout this work. A/1/1st Marines, for example, refers to A Company, 1st Battalion, 1st Marine Regiment; 2/7th Cavalry refers to 2nd Battalion, 7th Cavalry Regiment, and so on.

A note on measure

Units of measure are mostly given in metric in this work. A conversion table is provided below to assist the reader with the most common measures:

1mm	0.039 inches
1cm	0.39 inches
1m	1.09 yards
1km	0.62 miles
$1km^2$	0.38 square miles

PREVIOUS PAGE
Marines bring forward a stretcher for a wounded corpsman in Hue Citadel. (Bettman via Getty Images)

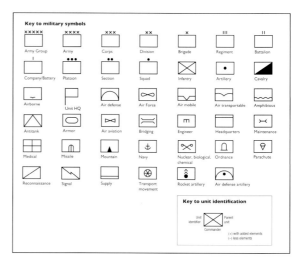

CONTENTS

ORIGINS OF THE CAMPAIGN

On March 8, 1965, elements of the US 9th Marine Expeditionary Force came ashore in Vietnam at Red Beach near Da Nang, ostensibly to provide security for the US air base there. A month later, President Lyndon Johnson authorized the use of US ground troops for offensive combat operations in Vietnam. These events marked a significant change in US involvement in the ongoing war between the South Vietnamese government and its Communist foes. Heretofore, US forces had been supporting the South Vietnamese with advisors and air support, but with the arrival of the Marines, a massive US buildup ensued that resulted in 184,300 American troops on the ground in Vietnam by the end of 1965. This number would rapidly increase until there were over 485,000 troops in-country by the end of 1967.

Eventually US ground troops were deployed in all four corps tactical zones (CTZs) and actively conducted combat operations against the Viet Cong (VC) and its North Vietnamese counterparts, the People's Army of Vietnam (PAVN – also known as the North Vietnamese Army or NVA). The first major confrontation between US forces and PAVN troops occurred in November 1965 in the battle of the Ia Drang Valley in the Central Highlands. Over the next two years, US forces conducted many large-scale search and destroy operations, such as *Masher/White Wing*, *Hastings*, *Cedar Falls*, and *Junction City*. These operations were designed to find and destroy the enemy forces in a war of attrition. However, by the end of 1967, the war in Vietnam had degenerated into a bloody stalemate. US and South Vietnamese operations had inflicted high casualties and disrupted Communist operations, but the North Vietnamese continued to infiltrate troops into South Vietnam and allied casualty rates increased weekly. Nevertheless, General William C. Westmoreland, Commander of US forces in Vietnam, was very optimistic that progress was being made; on November 21, 1967, he appeared before the National Press Club in Washington DC, and proclaimed: "We have reached an important point when the end begins to come into view. I am absolutely certain that, whereas in 1965 the enemy was winning, today he is certainly losing. The enemy's hopes are bankrupt." Subsequent events in 1968 would prove him wrong.

Meanwhile, in Hanoi, even as Westmoreland spoke, the Central Committee of the Lao Dong Party was finalizing preparations for a country-wide offensive in the south designed to break the stalemate and "liberate" South Vietnam. The decision to launch the offensive was the result of a long-standing internal struggle over military strategy within the party leadership in Hanoi. These struggles were principally over the timing involved in shifting

from a protracted war strategy toward a more decisive approach. In the end, however, the more cautious proponents of protracted war were overcome by Party First Secretary Le Duan and General Nguyen Chi Thanh, commander in the South, who advocated a nationwide general offensive.

The preparations for the offensive began in the summer months of 1967—the target date for launching the offensive was the beginning of Tet, the Lunar New Year holiday, which would come at the end of January 1968. Tet was the most important holiday of the year, when most South Vietnamese soldiers took leave to visit their families during a ceasefire scheduled in honor of the holiday. The Communists hoped to achieve complete surprise by launching their attack during the ceasefire.

During the second half of 1967, in what would today be called "shaping operations," the Communists launched a number of attacks to draw US and allied attention away from the southern population centers, which would be the ultimate objectives for the 1968 offensive. As part of this effort, PAVN forces from the 325C Division engaged the US Marines in a series of sharp battles in the hills surrounding Khe Sanh, a base in western Quang Tri Province, south of the demilitarized zone (DMZ) near the Laotian border.

Farther to the east, additional NVA forces besieged the Marine base at Con Thien just south of the DMZ in Quang Tri Province. Farther south, Communist forces attacked Loc Ninh and Song Be both in III CTZ, and in November they struck US forces at Dak To in the Central Highlands. In purely tactical terms, these "border battles," as they became known, were costly failures for the Communists and they no doubt lost some of their best troops, sustaining over 400 killed at Dak To alone. However, at the operational level, these battles achieved the intent of Hanoi's plan by diverting General Westmoreland's attention to the outlying areas away from the buildup around the urban target areas that would be the focus of the Tet attacks.

US military intelligence analysts knew that the other side was planning some kind of large-scale attack in 1968, but they did not believe that it would come during Tet or that it would be countrywide. Still, there were

US Marines double-time across an open field during a combat operation near Con Thien, Quang Tri Province, in late 1967. (USMC/DOD)

many indicators during the last few months of 1967 that something was afoot. When new intelligence poured in from all four corps tactical zones, Westmoreland and his staff came to the conclusion that a major enemy effort was probable—all signs pointed to a new offensive. Still, most of the significant enemy activity had been along the DMZ and in the remote border areas, rather than in the major populated areas.

In the words of one official in the Johnson White House, writing later in 1968, the Tet Offensive represented "the worst intelligence failure of the war." Many historians and other observers have endeavored to understand how the Communists were able to achieve such a stunning level of surprise. There are a number of possible explanations, but there are two main reasons for the failure to predict what was coming. First, allied estimates of enemy troop strengths and intentions were flawed. Part of the problem was that in the fall of 1967, Headquarters Military Assistance Command, Vietnam (MACV) in Saigon, in the face of vigorous disagreement from the Central Intelligence Agency, changed the way it calculated the enemy order of battle—that is, the enemy's estimated fighting strength and organization for combat. At Westmoreland's direction, the military analysts decided not to count the local militias of the National Liberation Front in the enemy order of battle, instantly reducing estimated enemy strength downward from 300,000 to 235,000. Almost overnight, this seemed to indicate that the war was going better than it was, but at the same time, this assessment discounted a large number of potentially effective enemy fighters and support personnel. Having revised their enemy estimates, it appears that US military intelligence analysts then apparently accepted those estimates at face value—as ground truth—this is tantamount to what is known in some military circles as "drinking your own bath water."

This caused Westmoreland and his analysts to give little credence to any intelligence indicators that ran counter to the prevailing assessment that the enemy was getting weaker and that any new offensive, because of this overall weakness, would be localized and limited. Thus, when incoming intelligence reports indicated that the enemy was planning a countrywide offensive, the reports were largely ignored or downplayed. While some analysts agreed that some type of offensive was possible following the Tet holiday, no one anticipated the nature and scope of the enemy offensive to come.

The second major reason for the failure to predict the size and scope of the offensive was the focus on Khe Sanh. In late December 1967, signals intelligence indicated that there was a significant enemy buildup in the Khe Sanh area, site of the earlier "Hill Fights;" elements of the 304th, 320th, and 325C PAVN divisions were identified in the area. Westmoreland and his intelligence analysts decided that this buildup signified that the enemy's main effort in 1968 would come at Khe Sanh. Therefore, Westmoreland, his headquarters, and the White House turned all their focus on Khe Sanh and the northernmost provinces.

On January 21, 1968, the North Vietnamese Army began the first large-scale shelling of Khe Sanh, which was followed by renewed heavy fighting in the hills surrounding the Marine base. These attacks seemed to confirm Westmoreland's assessment that the remote Marine base would be the focal point for any new Communist effort. He was sure that this was the opening salvo of the anticipated enemy offensive and a successful attack there could put the entire northern region at peril. The fact that the Khe Sanh situation looked hauntingly similar to that which the French had faced when they were decisively defeated at Dien Bien Phu in 1954 only added increased urgency to the events unfolding there; President Johnson declared that there would not be a replay of Dien Bien Phu at Khe Sanh and that the Marine base would be held at all costs.

Accordingly, Westmoreland ordered the commencement of Operation *Niagara*, a massive bombing campaign focused on suspected enemy positions around Khe Sanh. Additionally, he ordered the 1st Cavalry Division from the Central Highlands to Phu Bai just south of Hue and one brigade of the 101st Airborne Division to I Corps to strengthen the defenses in the northernmost provinces. By the end of January 1968, more than half of all US combat maneuver battalions were in the I Corps area.

THE TET OFFENSIVE

With all eyes on Khe Sanh, the North Vietnamese and Viet Cong forces made their final preparations for the coming general offensive. The time of attack was set for the early morning hours of January 31, 1968, to take advantage of the Tet ceasefire then in effect. Due to some confusion brought about by part of the force using a different lunar calendar, some attacks were launched prematurely just after midnight on January 30 against five province capitals in I and II CTZs. However, the preponderance of the attack went off as planned in the early morning hours of January 31. Altogether, the combined forces of the Viet Cong and the North Vietnamese Army, a total of over 84,000 troops, struck with a fury that was breathtaking in both its scope and suddenness. In attacks that ranged from the DMZ in the north all the way

The Tet Offensive 1968

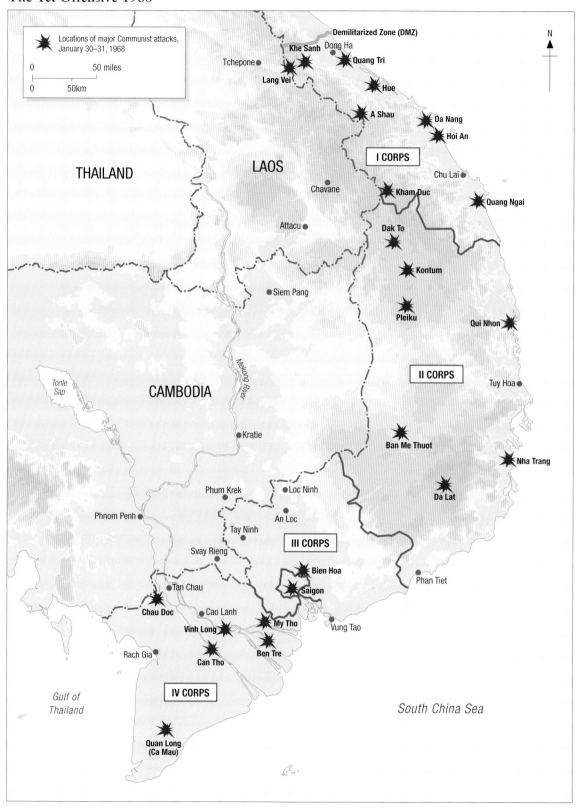

Locations of major Communist attacks, January 30–31, 1968

0   50 miles

0   50km

THAILAND

LAOS

Demilitarized Zone (DMZ)

N

Tchepone

Khe Sanh   Dong Ha

Lang Vei   Quang Tri

Hue

A Shau   Da Nang
                Hoi An

I CORPS

Chavane   Chu Lai

Kham Duc   Quang Ngai

Attacu   Dak To

Kontum

Siem Pang

Pleiku   Qui Nhon

II CORPS   Tuy Hoa

CAMBODIA

Tonle
Sap

Kratie   Ban Me Thuot

Nha Trang

Phum Krek   Loc Ninh

Phnom Penh   An Loc   Da Lat

Tay Ninh

III CORPS

Svay Rieng

Bien Hoa

Tan Chau   Saigon   Phan Tiet

Chau Doc   Cao Lanh

Vinh Long   My Tho

Rach Gia   Vung Tao

Ben Tre

Can Tho

IV CORPS

Gulf of
Thailand

South China Sea

Quan Long
(Ca Mau)

Mekong River

to the tip of the Ca Mau Peninsula in the south, the NVA and VC struck 36 of South Vietnam's 44 province capitals, five of its six largest cities, 71 of 242 district capitals, 50 hamlets, and virtually every allied airfield and key military installation in the country. One of the longest and bloodiest battles of the 1968 Tet Offensive was at Hue.

HUE CITY

The city of Hue was one of the most venerated places in Vietnam. Sitting astride Highway (QL) 1, 10km west of the coast and 100km south of the DMZ, Hue was the capital of Thua Thien Province and South Vietnam's third largest city, with a population of 140,000 in early 1968. The city was the old imperial capital and served as the religious, cultural, and intellectual center of Vietnam.

Revered by both sides, Hue had been treated almost as an open city by the VC and North Vietnamese Army and, except for occasional acts of terrorism by the Viet Cong, the city had remained remarkably free of war. Hue, however, was not without strategic importance; it was on one of the main land supply routes for the allied troops occupying positions along the DMZ to the north and it also served as a major unloading point for waterborne supplies that were brought inland via the river from Da Nang on the coast. Although there had been sporadic mortar and rocket attacks in the area by the local VC, Hue itself had been relatively peaceful and secure prior to Tet in 1968.

Hue was really two cities divided by the Song Huong, or River of Perfume, which flowed from the southwest to the northeast through the city on its way to the South China Sea 10km to the east. Two-thirds of the city's population lived north of the river within the walls of the Old City, or Citadel. Just outside the walls of the Citadel to the east was the densely populated district of Gia Hoi.

The Citadel was an imposing fortress, begun with the aid of the French in 1802 by Emperor Gia Long, the founder of the Nguyen Dynasty. Modeled on

The Imperial Palace of Hue, within the Citadel, built in the early 1800s by Gia Long, first emperor of the Nguyen Dynasty. (THIERRY ORBAN/ Sygma via Getty Images)

One of the gateways in Hue Citadel; these gates would prove very difficult to attack once the battle began. (Bettman via Getty Images)

Beijing's Forbidden City, it became the residence of the Annamese emperors who had ruled the central portion of present-day Vietnam.

The Citadel, a diamond-shaped, Vauban-style fortress with thick walls and high towers, included three concentric cities and a labyrinth of readily defensible positions. The outer perimeter of the Citadel was encircled by the Perfume, Dong Ba, Dao Cua Hau and Ke Van rivers, with only a handful of bridges crossing them. Each side of the Citadel measured *c*. 2.45km; three were straight, while the fourth was rounded slightly to follow the curve of the Perfume River. Beyond the four rivers on the Citadel side was a zigzag moat that was 27m wide at many points and up to 3.6m deep. The moat was protected by a rampart 9m high and up to 12m thick, with 13 gate towers restricting access to the Citadel within. Many areas of the outer perimeter were honeycombed with bunkers and tunnels that had been constructed by the Japanese when they occupied the city during World War II.

The Citadel, which encompasses an area of more than 7km^2, included block after block of row houses, parks, formal gardens, villas, shops, pagodas, and various buildings. Within the Citadel was another enclave, Hoang Thanh, or the Imperial Palace, where the Nguyen emperors had held court until 1883, when the French took control of Vietnam and ultimately the rest of Indochina. Located at the southeastern end of the Citadel, the palace was essentially a square with 6m-high walls that measured 700m per side. It contained a throne room constructed of intricately painted wooden beams and decorated with elaborate dragons. The palace grounds included a number of buildings and lush gardens. The entrance to the Palace was through the stately Ngo Mon (Midday) Gate, which was topped by a tall flagpole.

Also inside the Citadel walls was the Tay Loc Airfield, which had been added in modern times and would play a key role in the coming battle. To the east of the airfield, the Ngu Ha Canal cut through the Citadel and into the Thuy Quan and Thanh Long aqueducts outside the Citadel. Boats could enter and leave the Citadel by this canal.

South of the river lay the newer, more modern part of the city, which was about half the size of the Citadel and in which resided about a third of the city's population. The southern half of Hue, also known as the Triangle (formed by the Perfume River on the northwest, the Phu Cam River on the south, and a small stream called Phat Lac on the east), was linked to the Citadel by the Bach Ho railroad bridge in the west. To the east, highway QL 1 passed over the six-span Nguyen Hoang Bridge, an iron structure designed and built in 1897 by French engineering company Schneider et Letellier. This bridge had originally been named the Truong Tien Bridge, but was renamed in 1955 after the establishment of the Republic of Vietnam. On the southern edge of the modern city, QL 1 from the south crossed over the Phu Cam River on the An Cuu Bridge.

Key sites within Hue City

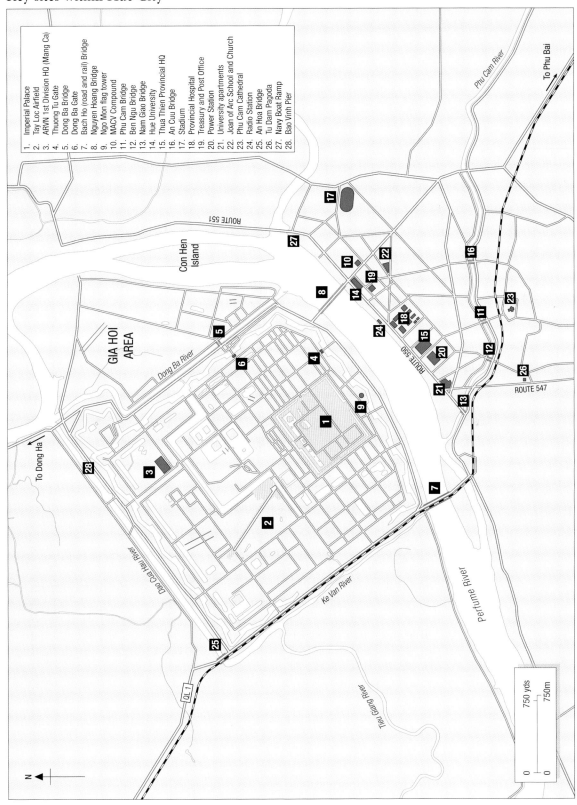

1. Imperial Palace
2. Tay Loc Airfield
3. ARVN 1st Division HQ (Mang Ca)
4. Thuong Tu Gate
5. Dong Ba Bridge
6. Dong Ba Gate
7. Bach Ho (road and rail) Bridge
8. Nguyen Hoang Bridge
9. Ngo Mon flag tower
10. MACV Compound
11. Phu Cam Bridge
12. Ben Ngu Bridge
13. Nam Giao Bridge
14. Hue University
15. Thua Thien Provincial HQ
16. An Cuu Bridge
17. Stadium
18. Provincial Hospital
19. Treasury and Post Office
20. Power Station
21. University apartments
22. Joan of Arc School and Church
23. Phu Cam Cathedral
24. Radio Station
25. An Hoa Bridge
26. Tu Dam Pagoda
27. Navy Boat Ramp
28. Bao Vinh Pier

The modern city included the provincial hospital, prison, the Catholic cathedral—the Church of the Most Holy Redeemer—and many of the city's modern structures, to include the Thua Thien Provincial Headquarters, government administrative buildings, the US Consulate, Hue University and the city's high school.

Three residential districts bordered the newer part of the city. They were Huong Tra, Phu Vang, and Huong Thuy. There were also a number of small villages near the city, including Dinh Mon and Duong Hoa, near the famous Gia Long Tomb, where the founder of the Nguyen Dynasty was buried. These areas would serve as staging enemies for the VC and NVA before the attack on the city.

The rural area surrounding Hue was mostly low, with slightly rolling hills and sparse scrub brush. Many stone tombs and peasant houses of mud and straw were scattered throughout the outskirts of the city, while the area to the west, north, and east was primarily characterized by continuous rice paddies.

During the early months of 1968 when the Battle of Hue occurred, the local weather was characterized by low ceilings, poor visibility, light rains, and morning fog. These conditions would greatly hamper air operations during the battle. The maximum and minimum temperatures during January and February averaged 69 and 60.2 degrees F respectively with an average humidity of 84.7 percent. Approximately 6.8cm of rain fell during the period.

When the battle began, there was not a large allied military presence in Hue. The 1st ARVN Infantry Division was headquartered in the northern corner of the Citadel in the fortified Mang Ca Compound, which was protected by 1.8–2.4m-high walls, topped by barbed wire. However, most of the division troops were spread out along QL 1, from Hue north toward the DMZ. At the time of the Tet attack, there were fewer than a thousand South Vietnamese soldiers in the city itself and many of them were on holiday leave visiting their families in the area.

The only US military presence in the city of Hue when the battle began was the MACV Compound, which housed about 200 US Army, US Marine Corps, and Australian officers and men who served as advisors to the 1st ARVN Division. They maintained a lightly fortified compound on the eastern edge of the modern part of the city about a block and a half south of the Nguyen Hoang Bridge. A small group of advisors were on duty at the Mang Ca Compound and other advisors stayed in the field with the units they advised. Also inside the modern city, a handful of US Army technicians manned a radar station and communications facility a few hundred meters to the west of the advisory compound. Lastly, a small detachment of US Navy personnel was stationed near the landing craft ramp on the south side of the river just north of the MACV Compound.

The nearest US combat base to Hue was at Phu Bai, 12.9km south along QL 1. Phu Bai was a major Marine Corps command post and support facility that was the home of Task Force X-Ray, which had been established as a forward headquarters of the 1st Marine Division. The task force, commanded by Brigadier-General Foster C. "Frosty" LaHue, Assistant Division Commander of the 1st Marine Division, was made up of two Marine regimental headquarters and three battalions. Most of these troops, including Brigadier-General Lahue, had only recently arrived in the Phu Bai area, having been displaced from Da Nang and other areas, and they were still getting acquainted with the area of operations when the Communists launched their attack on Hue.

CHRONOLOGY

1967

July 7	Central Committee of the Lao Dong Party in Hanoi decides to launch the General Offensive/General Uprising.
July 19	North Vietnamese delegation leaves Hanoi for Beijing on the first leg of a trip to secure additional weapons and other aid from Communist countries.
Late July	Viet Cong commanders meet in Cambodia to plan how to implement the General Offensive/General Uprising.
August	TF X-Ray is formed at Phu Bai.
September 3	Nguyen Van Thieu is elected president and Nguyen Cao Ky elected vice president of the Republic of Vietnam.
September 11–October 31	US Marines are besieged at Con Thien 3.2km south of the DMZ by North Vietnamese regulars; the fighting exacts an extremely heavy toll on both sides.
September 14–16	Defense Minister Vo Nguyen Giap of North Vietnam, in several radio broadcasts, endorses strategy of protracted war but declares "our fight will be more violent in the days ahead."
September 23	Soviet Union signs new aid agreement with North Vietnam in Moscow ceremony.
October 27	Battle of Song Be ensues when North Vietnamese forces attack the South Vietnamese base in Phuoc Long Province, near the Cambodian border in III Corps Tactical Zone.
October 29–November 3	Battle of Loc Ninh between 273rd Viet Cong Regiment and elements of the US 1st Infantry Division; VC attempt to hold district capital in Binh Long Province in III Corps Tactical Zone.
November 3–December 1	North Vietnamese regiments mass in the Dak To area in the Central Highlands, resulting in a series of bloody battles with elements of the US 4th Infantry Division and the 173rd Airborne Brigade.
November 6	Document captured by US forces near Dak To indicates battles in that area were meant to divert US forces to the mountainous areas while improving techniques of coordinated attacks.
November 16	General Westmoreland tells House Armed Services Committee that United States military withdrawal from Vietnam can begin within two years if progress continues.
November 17	National Liberation Front proclaims three-day ceasefires for Christmas and New Year, and seven-day ceasefire for Tet holiday.
November 19	US forces in Quang Tin Province capture Communist Party document ordering General Offensive and General Uprising.
November 21	At a speech at the National Press Club in Washington DC, General Westmoreland reports that progress is being made in the war and that the end is coming into view; predicts US troop withdrawals to begin in two years.
December 30	Messengers deliver Ho Chi Minh's Tet poem to officials and diplomats in Hanoi; Foreign Minister Nguyen Duy Trinh announces that North Vietnam would begin negotiations with the United States if bombing and other acts of war against the North were stopped.

December 31	US troop levels reach 485,600 with 16,021 combat deaths to date.	January 30	Communists launch surprise attacks on Nha Trang, followed by attacks on two cities in I Corps and five cities in II Corps; Brigadier-General Ngo Quang Truong cancels all leave in the ARVN 1st Division and puts his troops on alert.

1968

January 5	Operation *Niagara* begins with an intensive intelligence and surveillance effort directed against enemy buildup in the area around Khe Sanh.
January 10	General Westmoreland, after consultation with Lieutenant-General Frederick Weyand of II Field Force, orders redeployment of US forces to positions closer to Saigon.
January 13	Brigadier-General LaHue opens Task Force X-Ray headquarters in Phu Bai.
January 15	TF X-Ray assumes responsibility for the tactical area of operations from the 3rd Marine Division, which moves its headquarters to Dong Ha.
January 20	Marine battalion and NVA forces battle for control of the hills surrounding Khe Sanh Combat Base.
January 21	North Vietnamese forces overrun village of Khe Sanh and begin to shell the Marines at Khe Sanh Combat Base, initiating a 77-day siege; also on this day, MACV orders the commencement of Operation *Niagara II*, the concentrated bombing of enemy locations surrounding Khe Sanh Combat Base.
January 27	Communist seven-day Tet ceasefire begins; allied troops are restricted to their posts and all leaves are canceled under last-minute orders.
January 29	Tet celebration begins in North Vietnam; Tet ceasefire for allies is canceled in I CTZ, but ceasefire takes effect in rest of South Vietnam at 1800hrs.

January 31	Communists launch simultaneous attacks on major cities, towns, and military bases throughout South Vietnam; in Hue, the 4th PAVN Regiment takes over the New City south of the river, while the 6th PAVN Regiment captures the Citadel north of the river; Task Force X-Ray sends A Company, 1st Battalion, 1st Marines (A/1/1st Marines) to Hue.
February 1	Brigadier-General Ngo Quang Truong calls in reinforcements from his 3rd Regiment, the 1st ARVN Airborne Task Force and 3rd Troop, 7th Armored Cavalry; Brigadier-General LaHue orders 1/1st Marines to secure Thua Thien Provincial Headquarters and the prison.
February 3	Command groups of 1st Marines and 2nd Battalion, 5th Marines (2/5th Marines) arrive in Hue and launch attack to seize the public health building, Post Office, and Treasury facilities; elements of 3rd Brigade, 1st Cavalry Division begin movement toward Hue.
February 5	Marines resume attack toward city hospital and Provincial HQ; ARVN troops capture An Hoa Gate in the northwestern corner of the Citadel.
February 6	Marines capture the Provincial HQ and raise US flag; north of the river, NVA counterattacks against the 2nd Battalion, 4th ARVN Regiment.
February 7	Marines resume their advance; 3rd ARVN Regiment boards motorized junks and lands at the wharf; takes up positions in the Mang Ca Compound.

| February 10 | Marines secure all objectives south of the river and control that part of Hue City; General Cushman orders General LaHue to move a Marine battalion across the river to assist in clearing the Citadel. |

| February 12 | MACV Forward Headquarters is established at Phu Bai. |

| February 13 | Marine engineers build pontoon bridge over the Phu Cam River; 1/5th Marines launches attack southeast along the Citadel wall to clear enemy in assigned zone. |

| February 14 | 1/5th Marines resumes its attack. |

| February 15 | General Abrams assumes command of MACV Forward Headquarters at Phu Bai. |

| February 16 | General Abrams meets with Vice President Nguyen Cao Ky, Lieutenant-General Hoang Xuan Lam, Lieutenant-General Cushman, and Brigadier-General LaHue at MACV Forward Headquarters in Phu Bai. |

| February 17 | Record weekly total of US casualties set during preceding seven days: 543 killed and 2,547 wounded. |

| February 18 | 1st Brigade of the 101st Airborne Division is placed under the operational control of TF X-Ray. |

| February 21 | Platoon from A/1/5th Marines launches nighttime raid on administration building; rest of battalion attacks later that morning, securing the southern gate and surrounding wall by the end of the day. |

| February 24 | South Vietnamese troops storm former Imperial Palace in Citadel, tearing down the National Liberation Front flag and replacing it with the Republic of Vietnam flag. |

| February 25 | US and South Vietnamese troops retake control of Hue; there are 5,113 reported enemy casualties during the course of the bitter fighting in the city. |

| February 27 | CBS TV news anchorman Walter Cronkite, who has just returned from Saigon, tells American viewers during his CBS Evening News broadcast that he is certain "the bloody experience of Vietnam is to end in a stalemate." |

| March 31 | President Johnson announces in a nationally televised speech that he will order a unilateral halt to all US bombing north of the 20th Parallel and seek negotiations with Hanoi. He also announces his surprise decision not to seek re-election. |

| April 1 | The US 1st Cavalry Division (Airmobile) begins Operation *Pegasus* to reopen QL 9, the relief route to the Marine base at Khe Sanh. |

| December 31 | US military personnel in Vietnam number 536,000; 30,610 US military personnel killed in action to date. |

A Marine from A/1/1st Marines moves out under intense enemy fire during the heavy street fighting; he is supported by a 106mm recoilless rifle, which can be seen in the gateway to his right. (USMC/DOD)

OPPOSING PLANS

NORTH VIETNAMESE

There is still a lot that is unknown about the decision-making process in Hanoi that led to the Tet Offensive. However, it appears that deliberations began in the spring of 1967. Frustrated with the continuing bloody stalemate on the battlefield and concerned with the aggressive American tactics during the previous year, Communist leaders in Hanoi, led by Party First Secretary Le Duan and supported by General Nguyen Chi Thanh, commander of Communist forces in the South, decided to launch a general offensive to strike a major blow against the South Vietnamese and their US allies.

Le Duan hoped to achieve a "decisive victory" by combining widespread attacks with a general uprising by the South Vietnamese people, whom he believed could be convinced to rise and take up arms against the Saigon regime. Furthermore, he believed that the South Vietnamese forces were very weak and, when pressed, would collapse. His intention, he later acknowledged, was "to stretch the enemy throughout the Southern battlefield, drive his main force to battlefields advantageous to us and deal it crushing blows." With South Vietnamese forces defeated and the Saigon government toppled, the morale of the US forces would suffer and eventually the United States would withdraw from Vietnam.

Not everyone in the Hanoi hierarchy agreed with Le Duan. General Vo Nguyen Giap, PAVN commander-in-chief, believing that Communist forces were not strong enough to win a decisive victory against the combined American and allied forces, strongly advised against the proposed offensive. However, he was powerless against Le Duan and his followers, so Vo Nguyen Giap went into self-imposed exile in Hungary and would not return until after the offensive had run its course.

When General Nguyen Chi Thanh died unexpectedly, planning for the offensive continued under the direction of Vo Nguyen Giap's deputy, General Van Tien Dung. Under Van Tien Dung, the resulting campaign, called the General Offensive and General Uprising (*Tong Tien Cong va Noi Day Tet Mau Than*), was designed to break the stalemate and achieve three objectives: provoke a general uprising among the people in the South who would join the fight against Saigon, shatter the South Vietnamese armed forces, and convince the Americans that the war was unwinnable. The offensive would target cities and towns across South Vietnam, including Saigon, Da Nang, and Hue. The Communists prepared

for the coming offensive by a massive buildup of troops and equipment in the south.

Hue was particularly important to the planners in Hanoi. The city had played a central role in the confrontation in 1963 between the Buddhists and President Ngo Dinh Diem, a confrontation that ultimately led to a coup and Ngo Dinh Diem's death. For the next several years, Hue was the seat of militant Buddhists who continued to confront the regime in Saigon. Hanoi identified the political radicalism of the Buddhists with its own interests. As a result, the planners in Hanoi considered Hue to be the second most important objective, after Saigon, to be taken during the planned offensive. From their perspective, Hue would be the perfect place for the establishment of a coalition government in the south of their making.

Before the offensive began, the Communists prepared extensive plans for the attack on Hue, which would be directed by General Tran Van Quang, commander of the Tri-Thien-Hue sector. The plan, which would be executed by the newly formed Hue City Front, called for a division-size assault on the city, while other forces cut off access to the city from the north and south to preclude allied reinforcements from joining the battle. The main objective was to seize the city and surrounding towns and villages, set up a revolutionary administration, and repel any counterattacking forces. A history of the campaign published after the end of the war revealed that the attacking force was directed to annihilate the ARVN forces in and around Hue, primarily the 1st Infantry Division, while also striking at American forces in the city and those that might try to come to the relief of the ARVN force in the city from surrounding areas. D-Day was set for the early morning hours of January 31, 1968 to take advantage of the truce marking the beginning of the Lunar New Year, the Year of the Monkey.

While plans were made for the assault on the city, North Vietnamese logisticians stockpiled supplies in the mountain camps to the west and south of Hue. There, the enemy also established medical aid stations and hospitals staffed by both military and civilian personnel. At the same time, enemy combat units began to move toward the Hue area to occupy their attack positions.

Tran Van Quang and his senior commanders believed that once the city's population realized the superiority of the Communist troops, the people would immediately rise up to join forces with the VC and NVA against the Americans and the South Vietnamese, driving them out of Hue once and for all. Possessing very detailed information on civil and military installations within the city gleaned from patient observation and human informants, the Communist planners had divided the city into four tactical areas and prepared a list of 196 targets within the city. They planned to use all available soldiers to take the city in one swift blow.

Before the attack, Communist cadres would infiltrate the city, carrying false papers and wearing civilian clothes or South Vietnamese uniforms. They would smuggle their weapons into the city before the battle so they would be prepared to guide the assault troops when the attack began.

The attack under the Hue City Front would consist of two wings: the southern wing, the reinforced 4th NVA Regiment, would take the New City south of the Perfume River, and the northern wing, the 6th NVA Regiment reinforced with two battalions, would take the Citadel, to include the Mang Ca Compound in its northern corner, where the command post for the 1st ARVN Division was located. The northern wing would be the main attack. To support the seizure of Hue, assigned units would establish blocking positions along QL 1 to the north and south of the city to seal it off from outside reinforcement.

Communist documents captured during and after the Tet Offensive indicate that enemy troops received intensive training in the techniques of city street fighting before the offensive began. Extremely adept at fighting in the jungles and rice paddies, the NVA and VC troops required additional training to prepare for the special requirements of fighting in urban areas. This training, focusing on both individual and unit tasks, included tactics, techniques, and procedures to assist in taking the city, as well as defensive measures to help the Communists hold the city once they had seized it.

While the assault troops trained for the battle to come, VC intelligence officers prepared a list of "cruel tyrants and reactionary elements" to be rounded up during the early hours of the attack. This list included most South Vietnamese officials, military officers, politicians, American civilians, and other foreigners. After capture, these individuals were to be taken to the jungle outside the city where they would be punished for their crimes against the Vietnamese people.

The enemy had carefully selected the time for the attack. Because of the Tet holiday, the ARVN defenders would be at reduced strength. In addition, bad weather that traditionally accompanied the northeast monsoon season would hamper aerial resupply operations and

A US Marine aims his M60 at Communist troops along one of the Citadel's canals in February 1968. (Bettman via Getty Images)

impede close air support, which would otherwise give the allied forces in Hue a considerable advantage.

In preparation for the coming battle, the 6th NVA Regiment and the 12th Sapper Battalion that normally operated from the mountains northwest of Hue began moving toward the city. At the same time, the 5th NVA Regiment departed its base area in the Hai Lang Forest southwest of Quang Tri City and the 4th NVA Regiment began to move north from its operating area in the southern part of Thua Thien Province. For the coming attack, the Communists assembled a combined force that included eight infantry battalions, three sapper battalions, one rocket artillery battalion, two 82mm mortar companies, two 75mm recoilless rifle companies, two 12.7mm heavy machine-gun companies, and a number of local force companies—a total of over 10,000 soldiers. They were well equipped and had enough ammunition for an extended battle.

To draw allied attention away from the movement of these units towards Hue and other ongoing preparations for the main assault, Communist troops in the Phu Loc region southwest of Hue launched a series of diversionary attacks that began on January 7 and lasted for 20 days. These attacks were meant to divert allied attention away from Hue as the attacking forces moved to their assault positions around the city.

ALLIED

In late 1967, intelligence indicated that there was a buildup of enemy forces throughout South Vietnam, but especially in the northern border region of South Vietnam. There were reports of enemy divisions massed in the DMZ and also across the border in Laos. Seven North Vietnamese divisions had been identified operating within South Vietnam; five of these divisions were located in I and II CTZ. Additionally, there were major enemy artillery attacks against the Marine bases at Khe Sanh and Con Thien. To counter the growing threat in I CTZ, General Westmoreland (MACV commander, Vietnam) dispatched reinforcements to assist in the defense of the five northern provinces that made up I CTZ.

III Marine Amphibious Force (MAF), the senior US headquarters in the region, and I ARVN Corps, the senior South Vietnamese Army headquarters in the north, shared responsibility for the defense of the region. Prior to 1968, III MAF, a corps-level command, had under its control two reinforced Marine divisions, the 1st and 3rd; a US Army division, the Americal; the 1st Marine Air Wing; and the Force Logistics Command. The 3rd Marine Division and the 1st ARVN Division were responsible for the northern two provinces of Quang Tri and Thua Thien. The US Army's Americal Division and the 2nd ARVN Division operated in the southern provinces of Quang Tin and Quang Ngai. The 1st Marine Division and the 51st ARVN Regiment protected the central province of Quang Nam, which included Da Nang.

In late 1967, with reinforcements beginning to arrive in I CTZ, Lieutenant-General Robert E. Cushman, commander of III MAF, launched Operation *Checkers*, the realignment of Marine forces within the northernmost region. Under this plan, the 3rd Marine Division headquarters would deploy north from Phu Bai to Dong Ha and shift its forces north from Quang Nam and Thua Thien provinces to Quang Tri Province. The division would focus its

A US M42 Duster in the grounds of Hue University, February 9, 1968. The Duster tracked vehicle was armed with two 40mm antiaircraft guns, and was primarily used for convoy and base defense. (Bettmann via Getty Images)

efforts on the DMZ and westward to Khe Sahn. Meanwhile, the 1st Marine Division would take over responsibility for Thua Thien Province and reorient its forces to defend the corridor between Phu Bai and Da Nang. As part of this effort, the division would assume responsibility for defending the western approaches to Hue City.

By the beginning of 1968, elements of the 3rd Marine Division were positioned in a series of company-size strongpoints and battalion-size combat bases in northern Quang Tri Province to defend against a potential North Vietnamese attack across the DMZ, including Khe Sanh, Ca Lu, the Rockpile, Camp Carroll, Con Thien, and three bases strung along Route 566. Collectively, these formed a barrier known officially as the Strong Point Obstacle System, but more commonly known as the McNamara Line. In addition to the Marine bases, the McNamara Line also included thousands of acoustic and motion sensors to give the allies information about enemy infiltration into the area.

In early 1968, Army and Marine units in central and southern I CTZ under III MAF control attempted to continue operations as best they could as they shifted forces into newly assigned tactical areas to counter the ongoing enemy buildup. The repositioning of the Marine forces in Quang Tri and Thua Thien was only partially completed when the enemy launched the Tet Offensive.

While the Marines had begun repositioning, there was an enemy buildup around Khe Sanh. All evidence pointed to an impending attack on the remote Marine base there. At the same time, intelligence indicated the presence of the 5th and 341st NVA divisions in the Hue area. Other intelligence reports indicated a major enemy troop movement from the DMZ through Quang Tri Province into Thu Thien Province and a logistic buildup and other troop movements in the piedmont area west of Hue.

In view of these reports, on January 10, 1968, Westmoreland ordered the 1st Cavalry Division to reinforce the Marines in I CTZ. The 1st Brigade of the 1st Cavalry and the 2nd Brigade, 101st Airborne Division, temporarily attached to the 1st Cavalry, began redeploying north. The division quickly established an area of operation in southern Quang Tri and northern Thua

Thien provinces, occupying a series of firebases and landing zones between Phu Bai and Quang Tri City. The division was charged with protecting Quang Tri City from the south and southwest and preparing to launch an attack into enemy Base Areas 101 and 114, west of Hue. The nearest US Army unit to Hue itself was the 3rd Brigade, 1st Cavalry, operating from Camp Evans, 27km northwest of the city.

In January 1968, the 1st Marine Division had operational control of only two of its three regiments, the 5th and 7th Marines. As part of Operation *Checkers*, the division was given the responsibility for the Phu Bai Sector and elements of the 5th Marines deployed from Da Nang to the former 3rd Division tactical area of responsibility in the Phu Bai and Phu Loc sectors.

On January 11, 1st Marine Division activated TF X-Ray under Brigadier-General Foster C. LaHue and dispatched it to Phu Bai in Thua Thien Province to cover the western approaches to Hue City in coordination with the 1st ARVN Division. LaHue was given operational control of two regimental headquarters and three Marine battalions. The 5th Marines with two battalions would complete its relocation from Da Nang to the Phu Bai and Phu Loc sectors to assume responsibility for the southern half of the province extending to the Hai Van Pass. The 1st Marines with its 1st Battalion would assume control of the Phu Bai area of operations north toward Hue from the Truoi River.

On January 13, TF X-Ray assumed responsibility for its new area of operation. On January 15, the 3rd Marine Division commander moved his command post to Dong Ha, where he turned his focus on the DMZ and Khe Sanh.

Meanwhile, the South Vietnamese forces were stretched thin throughout I CTZ. The I ARVN Corps Commander assigned his best division, the 1st, to defend Quang Tri and Thua Thien provinces. The division's subordinate regiments were spread out in positions along QL 1. The 1st Regiment was stationed near Quang Tri City 50km to the northwest of Hue and the 2nd Regiment was another 12km farther up QL 1 near Dong Ha. Only one of the division's regiments, the 3rd, was stationed in Thua Thien Province; two of its battalions were conducting routine sweeps west of Hue and two battalions were searching for the enemy near the coast southeast of Hue. Also available to the 1st Division commander were two battalions of the South Vietnamese 1st Airborne Brigade and two troops of armored personnel carriers from the 7th ARVN Armored Cavalry located in a former French outpost on QL 1, 17km northwest of Hue.

As 1968 dawned, American intelligence reported that two North Vietnamese divisions were moving toward the Khe Sanh area and a third was located along the eastern DMZ. At the same time, captured enemy documents indicated major offensives throughout South Vietnam in the new year. General Westmoreland believed that the most logical objectives for a new attack in the northern provinces would be Khe Sanh and against key installations just south of the DMZ. He believed that the enemy planned to seize the two northern provinces and to make Khe Sanh the American Dien Bien Phu.

In further reaction to the enemy buildup in the northern region, on January 25, Westmoreland directed the establishment of a MACV Forward Headquarters in I CTZ. The forward headquarters would not be activated until mid-February, when it would assume operational control over all American forces in Quang Tri and Thua Thien.

OPPOSING COMMANDERS

ALLIED

American

In 1968, as previously stated, the commander of III Marine Amphibious Force was **Lieutenant-General Robert E. Cushman**. He was born in St Paul, Minnesota, on December 24, 1914. Cushman attended the United States Naval Academy, graduated tenth in his class in June 1935, and was commissioned a second lieutenant in the Marine Corps. His first duty assignment was in Shanghai, China, after which he served at naval shipyards in Brooklyn, New York, and Portsmouth, Virginia. Promoted to captain in March 1941, he was serving as the commanding officer of the Marine Detachment on the USS *Pennsylvania* when the Japanese attacked on December 7, 1941. He was subsequently transferred to the 9th Marine Regiment at San Diego in May 1942, embarking with the unit for the Pacific area in January 1943. Assuming command of 2/9th Marines, he and his unit saw action on Bougainville, Guam, and Iwo Jima.

Lieutenant-General Robert E. Cushman, USMC, commander of III Marine Amphibious Force during the 1968 Tet Offensive. (Bettman via Getty Images)

Upon his return to the United States in May 1945, he served at Marine Corps Schools in Quantico, Virginia, and at the Navy Department in Washington DC. He subsequently served in billets with the Central Intelligence Agency, Naval Forces Eastern Atlantic, the Armed Forces Staff College, and commanded the 2nd Marine Regiment at Camp Lejeune, North Carolina.

Cushman served four years as assistant for national security affairs to then-Vice President Richard Nixon. During that time, he was promoted to brigadier-general. Following that assignment, he served as the assistant division commander of the 3rd Marine Division on Okinawa. He was promoted to major-general in August 1961 and assumed command of the division.

After leaving the 3rd Division, Cushman subsequently served at Headquarters Marine Corps in Washington and from June 1964 until

March 1967, he was the commander of Marine Corps Base Camp Pendleton and, concurrently, commanding general, 4th Marine Division Headquarters Nucleus.

Cushman was posted to Vietnam in April 1967, where he was initially assigned as the deputy commander of III MAF, assuming command in June of 1967. At that time, III MAF was the largest combined combat unit ever led by a Marine.

As commander of III MAF, Cushman exercised direct control of two Marine divisions, the 1st and the 3rd. The commander of the 1st Marine Division was **Major-General Donn J. Robertson**. Robertson was born on September 9, 1916, in Willow City, North Dakota. He graduated from the University of North Dakota and was subsequently commissioned a second lieutenant in the Army Reserve in the summer of 1938. Robertson resigned his Reserve commission to accept appointment as a second lieutenant in the Marine Corps on June 1, 1938. During World War II he served in the 2nd and 5th Marine divisions. He commanded 3/27th Marines in the Battle of Iwo Jima; for his actions during that campaign, he received the Navy Cross, the US military's second highest decoration for valor.

Brigadier-General Foster C. LaHue, USMC, commander of Task Force X-Ray. (USMC/DOD)

In the years after the end of World War II, Robertson served in San Diego, Camp Pendleton, Marine Corps headquarters in Washington DC, at Guantanamo in Cuba, and Quantico, Virginia. He was posted to Korea in 1954, too late to see combat there. After that assignment, he returned to the Marine Corps staff in Washington and then the Fleet Marine Force Pacific in Hawaii. He was promoted to brigadier-general in 1963 and was assigned as commander of Fleet Marine Force Atlantic at Camp Lejeune, North Carolina.

Robertson was promoted to major-general in May 1967 and was reassigned to Vietnam, where he assumed command of the 1st Marine Division in June of that year. There, he directed a series of operations against the NVA in the Que Son Valley. Under Operation *Checkers*, he was directed to assume control of Thua Thien Province from Da Nang to Phu Bai from the 3rd Marine Division. In December 1967, in response to that directive, Robertson reactivated Task Force X-Ray, which had served as a temporary headquarters during a previous operation, and again placed his assistant division commander, **Brigadier-General Foster C. "Frosty" LaHue**, in command, charging him with protecting the western approaches to Hue City until the division could assume control of those operations directly.

Foster LaHue was born in Corydon, Indiana, on September 2, 1917. He attended DePauw University, graduating in 1939. He subsequently attended Officer Candidate School at Marine Corps Base Quantico, Virginia, in 1941 and was commissioned as a Marine second lieutenant in May of that year.

During World War II, LaHue saw action with the 1st and 4th Raider battalions, participating in the New Georgia and Admiralty Islands campaigns. During the Korean War, he served as the division adjutant for

1st Marine Regiment	Colonel Stanley S. Hughes
5th Marine Regiment	Colonel Robert D. Bohn
1st Brigade, 1st Cavalry Division	Colonel Donald V. Rattan
3rd Brigade, 1st Cavalry Division	Colonel Hubert S. Campbell
1st Brigade, 101st Airborne Division	Colonel John W. Collins, III
1st Battalion, 1st Marines	Lieutenant-Colonel Marcus J. Gravel
1st Battalion, 5th Marines	Major Robert H. Thompson
2nd Battalion, 5th Marines	Lieutenant-Colonel Ernest C. Cheatham, Jr

the 1st Marine Division before assuming command of the 3/1st Marines in June 1951.

After numerous schools and stateside assignments, LaHue was posted to Vietnam in March 1967, where he assumed the position of assistant division commander of the 1st Marine Division. As previously stated, Major-General Robertson formed Task Force X-Ray in August 1967 and placed LaHue in command. In Operation *Cochise*, LaHue led Task Force X-Ray against the 2nd NVA Division in the Que Son Valley, an area located at the boundary between Quang Nam and Quang Tin Province, which was considered to be the key to controlling Vietnam's northern region. However, the NVA managed largely to avoid contact with the three Marine battalions involved and the operation was terminated on August 28, 1967 with only modest results. After the termination of the operation, Task Force X-Ray was disestablished.

Task Force X-Ray was reactivated in December 1967, with LaHue again in command. He established his headquarters at Phu Bai Combat Base south of Hue and assumed operational control of the 1st and 5th Marine regiments. LaHue's would be the controlling Marine headquarters charged with retaking Hue after it was occupied by the North Vietnamese and VC forces.

When the battle for Hue began, LaHue assigned the mission of securing the city to **Colonel Stanley S. Hughes**, commander of the 1st Marine Regiment. He would assume overall tactical control of US forces in the city. Hughes, of Welsh, German, and Native American descent, was born in Elmira, New York, but grew up in Tioga County, Pennsylvania. He enlisted in the Marine Corps in 1940 and was subsequently selected for officer training. When World War II began, he shipped overseas with the 1st Marines. During the war in the Pacific, Hughes, then a first lieutenant in command of a machine-gun platoon in 3/7th Marines, was awarded the Navy Cross for action during the battle on Cape Gloucester, where he took over and led two rifle platoons when their lieutenants were killed. Later in the Battle of Peleliu as a captain in command of Company K of the 3rd Battalion, he was awarded the Silver Star and also received the Purple Heart for wounds sustained in combat. Hughes assumed command of the 1st Marines just before the Battle of Hue began. Older than other regimental commanders in the division, Hughes was well respected by his Marines.

South Vietnamese

The senior South Vietnamese commander in the northern region was **Lieutenant-General Hoang Xuan Lam**, commander of I ARVN Corps. Hoang

Xuan Lam was born in Hue on October 10, 1928. He was commissioned as a lieutenant of armored forces in 1951. He subsequently served in armor assignments of increasing responsibility until 1963 when he assumed command of the 23rd ARVN Division. In 1964, he assumed command of the 2nd ARVN Division.

Lieutenant-General Hoang Xuan Lam, commander of I ARVN Corps in 1968. (Bettman via Getty Images)

In 1967, due largely to his political connections with South Vietnamese President Nguyen Van Thieu, Hoang Xuan Lam was named commander of I ARVN Corps and given responsibility for I CTZ, an area that included five provinces: Quang Tri, Thua Thien, Quang Nam, Quang Tin, and Quang Ngai. Thus, Hoang Xuan Lam would oversee the battles for Khe Sanh, Quang Tri, and Hue in 1968. By the time of these battles, he had already established a reputation among his American counterparts for being less than aggressive.

As I Corps commander, Hoang Xuan Lam commanded two ARVN divisions, the 1st and 2nd. The commander of the 1st ARVN Division was **Brigadier-General Ngo Quang Truong**, regarded by many US advisors as one of the best senior commanders in the South Vietnamese armed forces. Ngo Quang Truong was born in Kien Hoa Province in the Mekong Delta on December 13, 1929. He graduated from My Tho College and attended the reserve officer school at Thu Duc in Saigon. He was commissioned as an infantry officer in the Vietnamese National Army (VNA) in 1954 (when the Republic of Vietnam was created in 1955, the VNA became the Army of the Republic of Vietnam, ARVN). After commissioning, he went to the airborne school at the Vietnamese National Military Academy in Da Lat. He served the next 12 years in the Airborne Brigade, gaining promotions through ability and combat leadership and not because of political influence or bribery, as was the case with many of his ARVN peers.

Lieutenant-General Ngo Quang Truong inspecting South Vietnamese troops in 1972; during the 1968 Tet Offensive, he was the commander of the 1st ARVN Division. (Bettman via Getty Images)

Ngo Quang Truong assumed command of the 5th Airborne Battalion in 1964 and led his paratroopers against two VC regiments, action for which he received a battlefield promotion to lieutenant-colonel. His reputation for valor and leadership under fire gained him the attention of senior generals in Saigon, including General Cao Van Vien, chief of the Joint General Staff.

During the Buddhist uprising that broke out in Hue in 1966, Ngo Quang Truong was ordered to put down the rebellion and regain control of the 1st ARVN Division, which had declared support for the

Buddhists. Although Ngo Quang Truong, a Buddhist himself, was less than comfortable with the mission, he commanded three airborne battalions that entered Hue and restored order, assuming temporary command of the 1st ARVN Division in the process.

The Joint General Staff was impressed with Ngo Quang Truong's performance and his appointment as commander of the 1st ARVN Division was made permanent. Ngo Quang Truong set about to turn the division into an effective fighting force. Over the course of the next year, the division became one of the best units in the South Vietnamese armed forces. Accordingly, Ngo Quang Truong was promoted to brigadier-general. His headquarters in the Citadel was one of the few military elements inside the city when the North Vietnamese and VC attacked.

NORTH VIETNAMESE

Tran Van Quang was born in Nghe An Province on the north central coast of Vietnam in 1917. He joined the Communist Party of Indochina in 1936. Between 1938 and 1939, he was one of the Communist party leaders in the Saigon area. He was incarcerated by the French in 1939, but escaped in October 1940. He traveled to Nghe An, but was recaptured by the French police and sentenced to life in prison. However, he was released in June of 1945.

From November 1946 to July 1947, Tran Van Quang was the Commissar of Inter-Region IV (which included 11 provinces of the north central Vietnamese coast). During the period 1948–49, Tran Van Quang was the military commander and political commissar of the Binh-Tri-Thien region. In May 1950, he joined the newly formed 304th Division as the political commissar.

In 1958, Tran Van Quang was promoted to major-general. In 1961, he went to southern Vietnam and became a member of the Central Executive Committee of the People's Revolutionary Party. In 1965, Tran Van Quang assumed command of the Tri-Thien-Hue military region, which was comprised of Quang Tri and Thua Thien provinces (and included the city of Hue). For the attack on Hue, Tran Van Quang formed the Hue City Front to directly control the action there.

Very little is known about the division and regimental commanders for both the VC and the NVA. One can reasonably assume that these officers, who had probably been fighting for a number of years, were combat hardened and well prepared for the coming fight.

OPPOSING FORCES

ALLIED

American

All US forces in South Vietnam were under the command of General William C. Westmoreland, commander of Military Assistance Command, Vietnam (MACV). By the beginning of 1968, there were nearly a half-million American soldiers, Marines, airmen, sailors, and coast guardsmen in-country. Additionally, Westmoreland controlled nearly 60,000 combat troops from South Korea, Australia, New Zealand, Thailand, and the Philippines, which were collectively known as Free World Military Assistance Forces.

For command and control purposes, the South Vietnamese Joint General Staff had divided Vietnam into four areas, designated Corps Tactical Zones, numbered I, II, III, and IV from north to south. Although this arrangement had been established by the South Vietnamese Joint General Staff, MACV adapted its command and control arrangements to this structure. There was no consolidated combined headquarters and the Americans and South Vietnamese had their own parallel, but separate, chains of command.

I Corps Tactical Zone, consisting of five provinces, was the northernmost military region in South Vietnam. The two most northern provinces in the region, Quang Tri and Thua Thien, were bordered on the north by the DMZ, on the south by Quang Nam Province, on the east by the South China Sea, and on the west by the Laotian border. The area was characterized by a narrow coastal plain, but most of the terrain to the west of the coast was dominated by hills and the Annamite Mountains.

At the beginning of 1968, III MAF, located at Da Nang, was a corps-level command that controlled more than 100,000 Marines, sailors, and soldiers. The Marine Corps divisions subordinate to III MAF were the 1st and 3rd divisions, plus 3,000 Marines from the 7th Fleet's two special landing forces that were attached to III MAF. The special

Under heavy enemy fire, US Marines deploy after helicopter insertion just south of the DMZ near the Laotian border in 1967. (Bettman via Getty Images)

I Corps Tactical Zone, January 30–31, 1968

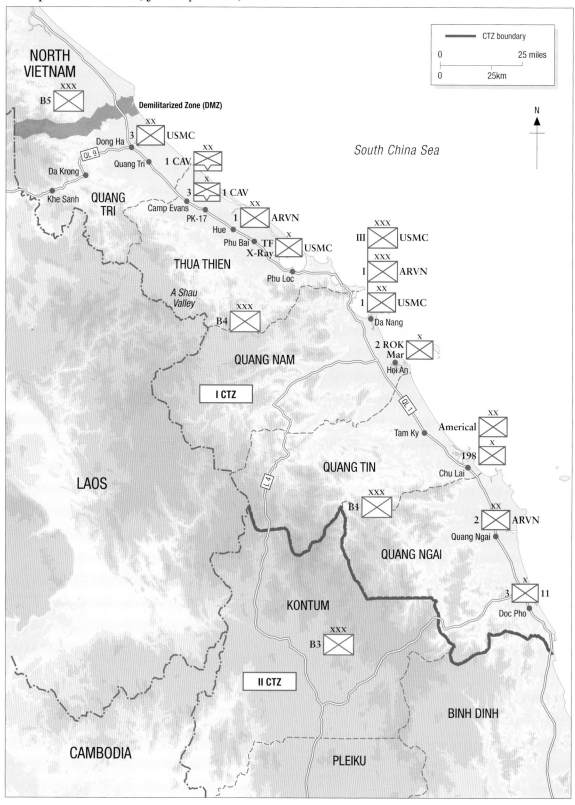

landing forces each consisted of a Marine battalion landing team (BLT), a battalion reinforced by supporting elements and a helicopter squadron. The Marine ground units were supported by the 1st Marine Air Wing based in Da Nang.

In addition to the Marine divisions and air wing, III MAF also controlled Force Troops, which included amphibian tractor and tank battalions, armored amphibian companies, and corps-level artillery. The division-sized Force Logistics Command provided logistical support to III MAF and its assigned and attached units.

Soldiers from the US 1st Cavalry Division leap from a helicopter during a sweep. (Bettman via Getty Images)

As the senior US headquarters in III CTZ at the beginning of 1968, III MAF also controlled the Army's 1st Cavalry Division (Airmobile), which had just been moved to the I Corps area, and the Americal Division (23rd Infantry), plus several separate and attached US Army brigades. The 1st Cavalry, commanded in 1968 by Major-General John J. Tolson III, was a light infantry division, but it had three organic aviation battalions, almost 400 helicopters, that allowed one-third of its infantry battalions to be lifted at one time. The division included nine battalions, which carried the traditional cavalry designations, but were really light infantry battalions each with an authorized strength of 920 men. Additionally, the 1st Cavalry included a division artillery of six battalions, an air cavalry squadron, and assorted other supporting arms. At the time of the Battle of Hue, two of the 1st Cavalry Division's brigades were scattered over a wide area from Phu Bai in the south to LZ (Landing Zone) Jane just south of Quang Tri in the north. The 1st Brigade of the 101st Airborne Division had recently been attached to the 1st Cavalry and had just arrived at Camp Evans (located north along QL 1 between Hue and Quang Tri), coming north from its previous area of operations. The brigade included two light infantry battalions, each with an authorized strength of 920 men.

III MAF also had operational control of the US Army 108th Artillery Group, which included a battalion of 105mm, self-propelled howitzers (18 tubes), a battalion of M42 "Duster" tracked vehicles armed with 40mm antiaircraft guns that were primarily used for convoy and base defense, and two battalions of 175mm guns (12 tubes in each battalion), several other artillery units and various combat support and combat service support elements.

In 1968 when the Tet Offensive began, the 3rd Marine Division, "The Fighting Third," headquartered at Dong Ha, was the primary American combat unit responsible for Quang Tri Province. Farther to the south was the 1st Marine Division, "The Old Breed," which was headquartered at Da Nang and had responsibility for Thua Thien Province and thus would direct the fight to retake Hue after it fell to the Communists.

The 1st Marine Division was activated in February 1941 and saw action in World War II at Guadalcanal, Peleliu, and Okinawa. In the Korean War, the division fought in the Pusan Perimeter, the Inchon landing, and the Battle of the Chosin Reservoir. At the time of the battle for Hue, the 1st Marine Division totaled 24,000 men, in five infantry regiments (its own 1st, 5th, and 7th regiments plus the attached 26th and 27th regiments from the 5th Marine Division), an artillery regiment, and supporting units.

In 1968, a typical Marine infantry regiment included a 222-man headquarters company and three infantry battalions. The regimental Headquarters & Service (H&S) Company was responsible for command, communications, and administration of the regiment; it included communications, antitank, and mortar platoons.

The basic tactical unit of the Marine regiment was the infantry battalion. Each battalion was organized into four 216-man rifle companies and a 385-man H&S company. The battalion H&S Company provided command, medical, supply, and administrative services for the battalion. It also included an antitank platoon and an 81mm mortar platoon.

The Marine rifle company was a small, self-contained combat unit; it included three 47-man rifle platoons. In addition, each company had a nine-man headquarters and a 66-man weapons platoon that included machine-gun, antitank, and light mortar sections. Each of the three rifle platoons had three rifle squads; each squad consisted of three four-man fire teams.[1]

The Marines were armed with a variety of individual and crew-served weapons. The standard weapon for the basic Marine rifleman was the 5.56mm M16A1 rifle. The 7.62mm M14 rifle was used as a long-range sniper weapon and was a weapon of choice for some Marines. Other weapons in the rifle platoons included the M79 40mm grenade launcher, M26 and M26A1 fragmentation grenades, and M18 Claymore mines.

Crew-served weapons that were found in the Marine infantry units included the 7.62mm M60 machine gun and the M2 .50-caliber heavy machine gun. Indirect fire weapons included the M19 60mm mortar and the M29 81mm mortar. Antitank weapons included the M20A1 3.5-inch rocket launcher (better known as the 'bazooka"), the 66mm M72 Light Antitank Weapon (LAW), and the M40A1 106mm recoilless rifle.

During the course of the battle for Hue, the Marines would be supported by several types of armored vehicles. The M50 Ontos, which mounted six 106mm recoilless rifles along with a .50-caliber spotting rifle, and the M48A3 Patton tank armed with a 90mm main gun and two machine guns, would both play key roles in the intense battle to retake Hue from the NVA and VC.

In addition to armored support, the Marine infantry could also count on indirect fire support from a number of heavy mortars and various types of artillery weapons, to include 105mm, 155mm, and 8-inch howitzers assigned to the Marine division artillery, and separate artillery batteries located at other echelons.

The command and control arrangements for the Marines in the

A US M50 Ontos and a laden M55 US Army gun truck prepare to move out in southern Hue City. The Ontos mounted six 106mm recoilless rifles along with a .50-caliber spotting rifle. The M55 was armed with quad .50-caliber machine guns. (Peter Balsiger/RDB/ullstein bild via Getty Images)

1 The numbers listed reflect the authorized unit strengths, but the Marines in Vietnam more often than not were understrength due to casualties, etc.

Battle of Hue conformed to common Marine practice, which was to task-organize battalions under regimental headquarters. Under this system, battalion-sized infantry units might be placed under the operational control of another formation, but not permanently transferred. That meant that a regimental headquarters might or might not operate with its own "normal" organic battalions; in fact, a regimental headquarters might be assigned responsibility for a specific tactical area of operation and assigned subordinate battalions "on loan," but have none of its assigned battalions under its command. Under this system of "opcon" or "operational control," the interchange of battalions between regimental headquarters was common. In some cases, the controlling headquarters might even be an ad hoc headquarters established for a specific task.

A good example of this approach was Task Force X-Ray, which had first been established in August 1967 for Operation *Cochise*. In early 1968, Task Force X-Ray was re-established and formed at Phu Bai as an advance element of the 1st Marine Division headquarters to serve temporarily as the main headquarters shifted its tactical area of responsibility from Quang Tri to Thua Thien Province under Operation *Checkers*.

When the battle for Hue began, Task Force X-Ray would take command of available units that were either caught in transit or were hastily dispatched from outlying areas in order to respond to the developing situation in Hue once the offensive began. Over the course of the battle, the commander of Task Force X-Ray would have operational control of the 1st Battalion of the 1st Marines; 1st and 2nd battalions and L Company of the 3rd Battalion, 5th Marines; 1st and 2nd battalions of the 11th Marines (artillery); a tank platoon and an antitank platoon from the 3rd Tank Battalion; 1st Engineer Battalion; 1st and 3rd Motor Transport battalions; 1st Shore Party Battalion; 7th Communications Battalion; 1st MP Company; and assorted other support platoons and detachments.

South Vietnamese

The South Vietnamese forces, which numbered about 685,000 military personnel, were controlled by the South Vietnamese Joint General Staff, which exercised command of the Army of the Republic of Vietnam (ARVN) through four subordinate corps headquarters. Each ARVN corps headquarters was responsible for an assigned geographic region (the CTZs) and had two or three ARVN infantry divisions attached. In addition to the divisions assigned to the respective corps headquarters, there was a strategic reserve made up of the Airborne Division and the Marine Division, which were not permanently attached to any corps headquarters and normally responded to orders directly from the Joint General Staff.

The senior ARVN headquarters in the area of operations that included Hue was I Corps, commanded by Lieutenant-General Hoang Xuan Lam. His command included two ARVN divisions: the 1st Division was headquartered in Hue and would be the senior ARVN headquarters inside the city during the fighting; and the 2nd Division, which was stationed in Quang Ngai Province. Hoang Xuan Lam also controlled the 51st Independent Regiment at Hoi An and the 54th Independent Regiment at Tam Ky. Additionally, Hoang Xuan Lam had operational control of several South Vietnamese Ranger battalions, three Vietnamese Airborne battalions and Vietnamese Marine Task Force Alpha, consisting of three battalions of Vietnamese Marines, from the general

ARVN soldiers wade a river while conducting combat operations against the Viet Cong. (Christopher Jensen/Getty Images)

reserve. I Corps forces also included a corps artillery unit with two 105mm battalions and six 155mm battalions, an engineer group with three battalions, an area logistical command, and several armored cavalry regiments.

The province chiefs in I Corps also answered to Lieutenant-General Hoang Xuan Lam, which meant that he controlled the Regional and Popular Forces (provincial militia) from the five provinces in the region, bringing the total number of troops at his disposal in 1968 to some 80,000 troops.

The 1st Division was a typical ARVN division that, in 1968, had an authorized strength of 10,450 men. It was normally comprised of a division headquarters company, three infantry regiments, division artillery of three M101A1 105mm battalions and one M114A1 155mm battalion, and an armored cavalry squadron equipped with M41A3 Walker Bulldog tanks and M113 armored personnel carriers. Additionally, the division included an engineer battalion, as well as reconnaissance, signal, transportation, ordnance, quartermaster, medical, and administration companies plus a military police detachment. The 1st ARVN Division was assisted by Advisory Team 3, a division combat assistance team made up of US and Australian advisors that was headquartered in Hue south of the Perfume River.

The infantry regiments of the 1st Division each included four infantry battalions. Each battalion contained a headquarters company and three rifle companies. Each rifle company consisted of three rifle platoons each with three 10-man rifle squads plus a weapons platoon, which included machine-gun, mortar, and rocket-launcher sections. The headquarters company of each regiment had service, medical, transportation and maintenance, mortar and recoilless rifle platoons, and a communication section.

Infantry soldiers in the ARVN battalions were similarly armed to their US counterparts, but did not have all the heavy weapons found in the American units. The basic weapon of the ARVN soldier was the M16A1 rifle; however, some ARVN soldiers carried the M1A1 Thompson submachine gun or the M3A1 "grease gun." Other weapons included the M60 machine gun, M79 grenade launcher, M18A1 57mm and M67 90mm recoilless rifle, M19 60mm mortars, M29 81mm mortars, and M20A1 3.5in rocket launchers.

During the course of the battle for Hue, Brigadier-General Ngo Quang Truong, commander of the 1st ARVN Division, would not have all of his own organic battalions available for the battle, because they were committed elsewhere when the Tet Offensive began. However, during the battle, he would have under his command an airborne task force, a South Vietnamese Marine task force, and a ranger task force. The 1st Airborne Task Force consisted of the 2nd, 7th, and 9th ARVN Airborne battalions. Marine Task Force Alpha included the 1st, 4th, and 5th battalions and the Ranger Task Force included the 21st and 39th Ranger battalions. The South Vietnamese paratroopers and Marines were considered to be among the best ARVN troops. They were similarly armed and equipped to the regular ARVN troops.

THE NVA AND VC

The Communist forces during the Battle of Hue included both the *Quan Doi Dang Dan*, People's Army of Vietnam (PAVN)—the regular army of the Democratic Republic of Vietnam, more popularly known at the time as the North Vietnamese Army, or NVA—and the *Quan Doi Giai Phong Nhan Dan*, People's Liberation Armed Forces (PLAF)—the armed insurgent force in South Vietnam, more popularly known as the Viet Cong (VC).

The genesis of the People's Army of Vietnam can be traced back to the armed propaganda groups that fought the Japanese under Vo Nguyen Giap during World War II and evolved into the *Viet Nam Doc Lap Dong Minh Hoi*, or Viet Minh, which fought against the French in the First Indochina War that developed in the years after Japan surrendered. Following the French defeat at Dien Bien Phu in 1954, Vo Nguyen Giap organized the Viet Minh into a modern fighting force to protect the homeland, resulting in the formation of the People's Army of Vietnam. This force evolved into a hybrid organization that included three tiers. At the bottom of the scale were the local militia at the district and village level. At the regional or provincial level, there were regional forces. At the top of the triangle, there were *Chu Lac*, or regular forces, which formed the main conventional forces for both the defense of North Vietnam and the liberation of the South. Over time, this force was modernized with the weapons and equipment provided by the People's Republic of China, the Soviet Union, and other Warsaw Pact members.

By the end of 1967, the PAVN had increased to 447,000 men and women organized into ten infantry divisions, an artillery division, an antiaircraft division, and over a hundred independent regiments. These were conventional military organizations, which were manned, trained, and equipped in North Vietnam and then moved south to take part in the war there.

The Central Committee of the Vietnam Workers' Party (*Dang Lao Dong Viet Nam*) in Hanoi formed and controlled the People's Revolutionary Party (PRP) in South Vietnam. The PRP in turn controlled the *Mat Tran Dan toc Giai Phong Mien Nam Viet Nam*, the National Front for the Liberation of South Vietnam, or as it was more commonly known, the National Liberation Front (NLF). The NLF was both a political organization and an armed insurgent force that exercised control over the People's Liberation Armed Forces, or Viet Cong, as they were more commonly known by the allied forces.

People's Army of Vietnam (North Vietnamese Army) troops conduct training near Bach Dang, near Hanoi, before moving down the Ho Chi Minh Trail to join the war in the South. (STF/AFP via Getty Images)

Troops of the People's Liberation Armed Forces, better known as the Viet Cong, marching toward the front to engage US and South Vietnamese forces. (Sovfoto/ Universal Images Group via Getty Images)

The VC were organized similarly to the PAVN with a triangular arrangement. The apex of the VC organization comprised the main-force units, which were manned by full-time soldiers, many of whom had been trained in the North and infiltrated south. These forces, also known as mobile forces, normally operated at the battalion level, but could join to form multi-battalion forces for particular campaigns.

Just below the main-force formations were the regional or territorial forces. These were also full-time soldiers, but, unlike the main-force units, these were primarily composed of locally recruited and trained soldiers who normally operated in the areas in which they were recruited. They usually worked as company-sized units, but could also join together for particular campaigns.

The final category of VC soldiers were local militia units, who were organized at the village and hamlet levels. These forces were aptly described as "farmers by day and soldiers by night." They operated in groups that ranged from small three-man cells to platoons. They could conduct some military operations, but were most often involved in supporting the regional and main-force units and in collecting intelligence, sabotage, assassination, and other low-level insurgent activities.

Under the initial command and control arrangement, the Communists established Military Region V to control NVA and VC operations in I and II Corps (Central Highlands). However, they separated the two northern provinces of Quang Tri and Thua Thien from Military Region V to form a new region, called the Tri-Thien-Hue Front. This region came directly under the North Vietnamese high command, rather than the Central Office of South Vietnam (COSVN), which controlled military operations in the southern two-thirds of the country.

As the Communists continued to plan for the general offensive, they created a new headquarters called the Hue City Front to direct the battle for the city. The new headquarters was staffed by high-ranking officials from the Tri-Thien-Hue Front, local party members, and military officers from the units involved in the attack. The Hue City Front would have authority over the battle for the city and the three districts that surrounded it. The enemy also created a rear services group that would keep supplies flowing into the battle area from the Communist mountain bases to the west.

When the battle for Hue began, the Hue City Front commanded 10,000 Communist troops, a total of ten battalions, including three NVA regiments of two or three battalions each. Most of these forces were highly trained North Vietnamese regular army units that had come south either across the DMZ or more likely, down the Ho Chi Minh Trail and in to the south from Laos and/or Cambodia. NVA infantry regiments at full strength had 2,500 troops organized into three infantry battalions and supporting arms. The battalions were normally organized into three companies; companies normally included three rifle platoons and a weapons platoon.

There was no standard allocation of weapons in the NVA or VC, but normally the infantrymen were armed with 7.62x39mm assault rifles, usually of the Chinese Type 56, which was an identical copy of the Soviet AK-47. Other standard infantry weapons included 7.62mm RPD light machine guns, and RPG-2 or RPG-7 (B-40, B-41) rocket launchers. In addition, infantrymen customarily were each armed with three to five Chinese Type 67 stick grenades. To support the infantry assault elements, the Communist forces had 107mm, 122mm, and 140mm free-flight rockets; 60mm, 82mm and 120mm mortars; 57mm and 75mm recoilless rifles, and several models of heavy machine guns, such as the 12.7mm DShKM38/46.

The North Vietnamese units that attacked Hue were joined by six Viet Cong main force battalions, including the 12th and Hue City Sapper battalions. A typical main-force VC infantry battalion consisted of 300–600 veteran, skilled fighters. The VC soldiers were armed similarly to the NVA with the exception that some VC soldiers carried the semi-automatic 7.62x39mm Chinese Type 52 rifle, a copy of the Soviet SKS, instead of the AK-47, and they did not have many of the heavier weapons that the NVA employed.

Viet Cong prisoners captured by allied forces during the Battle of Hue. (Bettmann via Getty Images)

During the course of the battle for Hue, the total Communist force in and around the city would grow to 20 battalions when elements from three additional infantry regiments were dispatched to the Hue area from the Khe Sanh battlefield.

ORDERS OF BATTLE, HUE CITY, JANUARY 31–MARCH 2, 1968

ALLIED

US FORCES

III Marine Expeditionary Force (USMC)
1st Marine Division
    Task Force X-Ray
        TF Headquarters and Headquarters Company
        Detachment, Headquarters Battalion, 1st Marine Division
        1st Counter-Intelligence Team
        Section, 2nd Special Security Communications Team
        Detachment, 1st Dental Company
        7th Intelligence Team
        13th Interrogator-Translator Team
        Detachment, 3rd Interrogator-Translator Team
        7th Antiaircraft Platoon, 29th CA Company (USA)
        B Company (-), 3rd Shore Party Battalion (February 22–29, 1968)

C Company (Reinforced), 1st Medical Battalion
Communication Company (-) (Reinforced), 7th Communication Battalion
1st Force Recon Company (Reinforced)
    1st Force Reconnaissance Company
    C Company, 1st Reconnaissance Battalion
    Platoon, D Company, 1st Reconnaissance Battalion
Battery D, 1st Battalion, 44th Artillery (Automatic Weapons, Self-Propelled) (USA)
1st Marine Regiment (Reinforced)
    Detachment, Headquarters Company
    Detachment, 3rd Interrogator-Translator Team
    1st Battalion, 1st Marines (-) (Reinforced)
        Detachment, Headquarters Company, 1st Marines
        A Company
        B Company (-)
    1st Battalion, 5th Marines
        Detachment, Headquarters & Service Company

A Company
B Company
C Company
D Company
L Company, 3rd Battalion, 5th Marines
2nd Battalion, 5th Marines
Detachment, Headquarters & Service Company
F Company
G Company
H Company
A Company, 1st Tank Battalion (-)
Anti-Tank Company, 1st Tank Battalion (-)
B Company, 1st Shore Party Battalion
A Company (-) (Reinforced), 1st Engineer Battalion
1st Platoon, B Company, 1st Engineer Battalion
B Company, 1st Motor Transport Battalion
3rd Tank Battalion
1st Field Artillery Group
1st Battalion (-) (Reinforced), 11th Marine Artillery Regiment
2nd Battalion (Airborne), 320th Artillery
108th Artillery Group (USA)
8th Battalion, 4th Artillery (175mm/8-inch, Self-Propelled)
1st Battalion, 44th Artillery (Automatic Weapons, Self-Propelled)
2nd Battalion, 94th Artillery (175mm/8-inch, Self-Propelled)

US Army
1st Cavalry Division (Airmobile)
1st Brigade
1st Battalion (Airmobile), 5th Cavalry
1st Battalion (Airmobile), 8th Cavalry
1st Battalion (Airmobile), 12th Cavalry
1st Battalion (Airborne), 502nd Infantry (attached)
3rd Brigade
1st Battalion (Airmobile), 7th Cavalry
5th Battalion (Airmobile), 7th Cavalry
2nd Battalion (Airmobile), 12th Cavalry
1st Brigade, 101st Airborne Division (OPCON TF X-Ray
February 22–March 2, 1968)
A Company (-), 326th Engineer Battalion
Security Platoon (-)
Aviation Section
Military Police Platoon (-)
Detachment (-), 181st Military Intelligence Battalion
406th Radio Research Detachment
Tactical Air Control Party (-)
Detachment, 20th Chemical Company
2nd Battalion (Airborne), 327th Infantry
2nd Platoon, A Company, 326th Engineer Battalion
A Company
B Company
C Company
Recon Platoon
2nd Battalion (Airborne), 501st Infantry
A Company
B Company
C Company
Recon Platoon
B Company, 1st Battalion, 5th Marines (February 26–
March 2, 1968)
2nd Battalion (Airborne), 320th Arty (DS)
A Company (-), 326th Engineer Battalion
Tactical Air Control Party (-)
Detachment, 20th Chemical Company
1st Squadron, 9th Cavalry
229th Aviation Battalion

ALLIED FORCES

Australian
1st Australian Advisory Group
Army of the Republic of Vietnam
I Corps
1st Infantry Division
1st Battalion
2nd Infantry Regiment
4th Battalion
3rd Infantry Regiment
1st Battalion
2nd Battalion
3rd Battalion
4th Battalion
Hac Bao ("Black Panther") Company
Reconnaissance Company
7th Armored Cavalry Squadron
1st Troop
2nd Troop
3rd Troop
1st Airborne Task Force, ARVN Airborne Division
2nd Airborne Battalion
7th Airborne Battalion
9th Airborne Battalion
Marine Task Force Alpha, Vietnamese Marine Division
1st Battalion
4th Battalion
5th Battalion
Ranger Task Force
21st Battalion
39th Battalion
Thua Thien Sector Troops (Regional Forces/Popular Forces)

PEOPLE'S ARMY OF VIETNAM (NVA)/PEOPLE'S LIBERATION ARMY (VC)

B4 OR TRI-THIEN-HUE FRONT

Hue City Front
4th PAVN Regiment
804th Battalion
810th Battalion
1st Sapper Battalion
5th PAVN Regiment
815th Battalion
818th Battalion
2nd Sapper Battalion
6th PAVN Regiment
800th Battalion
802nd Battalion
806th Battalion
12th Sapper Battalion
6th Battalion, 24th Regiment, 304th PAVN Division
7th Battalion, 29th PAVN Regiment, 325C PAVN Division
99th Regiment, 324B PAVN Division
164th PAVN Artillery Regiment
Hue City Sapper Unit

THE BATTLE OF HUE

PRELUDE TO THE BATTLE

The Tet holiday truce went into effect at 1800hrs on January 29. However, because of widespread truce violations by the enemy, MACV and the South Vietnamese Joint General Staff officially terminated the Tet holiday ceasefire on January 30. Shortly after midnight, there were a series of enemy attacks on Da Nang, Nha Trang, Qui Nhon, Tuy Hoa, and several other South Vietnamese installations along the central coast. The North Vietnamese plan called for the countrywide attack to begin on the first night of the Lunar New Year. However, North Vietnam's Maritime Meteorological Department adjusted its lunar calendar, moving the date of the new year one day forward. Word of this change reached only the coastal areas of central Vietnam. As a result, Communist forces in this area launched their attacks 24 hours ahead of the attacks in the rest of the country.

Brigadier-General Ngo Quang Truong, commander of the 1st ARVN Division, learned of these attacks the next morning, Lunar New Year's Day. At the same time, First Lieutenant Nguyen Thi Tan, commander of Truong's division reconnaissance company, reported that one of his patrols had observed an enemy force about 4km southwest of Hue; this force, estimated to be about two battalions, was reportedly headed toward the city (this was probably two battalions from the 6th PAVN Regiment). At 2200hrs that night, a Regional Force (RF) company to the east of Ngo Quang Truong's recon patrol was also attacked by a large enemy force. Additional intelligence reports indicated that there was an ongoing buildup of enemy troops 20km west of Hue. At the same time, enemy units had been harassing the Phu Loc area to the south of the city.

Brigadier-General Ngo Quang Truong, concerned with the enemy buildup in his area of operations, gathered his division staff at the headquarters in the Mang Ca Compound inside the Citadel and began making hasty measures to prepare to defend against what might come next. Unfortunately, over half of the division's troops were already on holiday leave and away from their units. Ngo Quang Truong put his remaining troops on full alert, confining them to the barracks. As for himself, the general decided to remain at his headquarters that night, rather than spend the holiday at his home south of the river in the New City.

Believing that the Communists would not attack the "open" city directly and that the most likely enemy course of action would be to strike in the

Elite South Vietnamese "Hac Bao" (Black Panther) troops conduct a combat assault in the A Shau Valley in 1967; the company would play a key role in the battle for the Citadel in Hue in 1968. (Bettman via Getty Images)

Phu Loc area to cut QL 1, Ngo Quang Truong had positioned the forces around the city to defend outside the urban area. The only units inside the city were the division's 36-man reconnaissance platoon and the elite Hac Bao "Black Panther" Company, commanded by Lieutenant Tran Ngoc Hue.

Ngo Quang Truong's closest units to the city were a troop from the 7th Armored Cavalry Squadron located at the Tam Thai military camp at An Cuu, 2km to the southeast of the Triangle, and the 3rd ARVN Regiment with two battalions, which was operating 8km to the west of the city. Two more of the regiment's battalions were operating southeast of the city near the coast. The 2nd and 7th Airborne battalions, attached to the 1st ARVN, and another troop from the 7th Armored Cavalry Squadron were operating from a temporary base called PK-17 10km northwest of Hue along QL 1. There was also a South Vietnamese engineer battalion camp about 2km southwest of the city. Additionally, there were several Regional Forces companies and Popular Forces platoons scattered throughout the surrounding villages and hamlets.

The only US military presence in Hue when the battle began was the aforementioned MACV Compound, which housed about 200 US Army, US Marine Corps, and a handful of Australian officers and men who served as advisors to the 1st ARVN Division. They maintained a lightly fortified compound on the eastern edge of the modern part of the city south of the river about a block and a half south of the Nguyen Hoang Bridge. A small group of advisors and Marine guards were on duty at the Mang Ca Compound and other advisors stayed in the field with the units they advised, to include a rotating group of staff personnel stationed at Brigadier-General Ngo Quang Truong's headquarters. Also inside the modern city, a handful of US Army technicians manned a radar station and communications facility a few hundred meters to the west of the advisory compound. Lastly a small detachment of US Navy personnel was stationed near the Navy LCU (landing craft utility) ramp on the south side of the river just north of the MACV Compound.

The closest US combat units were located to the southeast of Hue. The 2nd Battalion, 501st Infantry, a unit from the 101st Airborne Division attached to the 1st Cavalry Division, was defending the division's rear logistical base at LZ El Paso, 7km southeast of the Citadel along QL 1. Task Force X-Ray, a brigade-size task force from the 1st Marine Division, and its attached elements from the 1st and 5th Marine regiments operated from Phu Bai, 15km southeast of Hue. Twenty-five kilometers northwest of the Citadel, the 1st Cavalry's 3rd Brigade operated out of Camp Evans.

Despite Ngo Quang Truong's concerns about an enemy buildup in the area, Lunar New Year's Day in Hue passed without further incident amid the traditional holiday celebration. Still, he dispatched half the Hac Bao Company south of the river to secure the Thua Thien Provincial Headquarters just in case.

Unknown to Ngo Quang Truong as he made his preparations for whatever was to come, there was clear indication that there would be a direct attack on his city. On the day before the South Vietnamese commander put his staff on alert, a US Army radio intercept unit at Phu Bai overheard Communist orders calling for an imminent assault on Hue. Following standard procedure, the intercept unit forwarded the message through normal channels. Making its way through several command layers, the intercept and associated intelligence analysis did not make it to the Hue defenders, including US advisors at the MACV compound south of the river, until the next day when the city was already under attack.

Even as the intelligence report made its way slowly through channels, the Viet Cong had already infiltrated the city. Communist sappers had donned civilian clothing or ARVN uniforms and mingled with the throngs of people who had come to Hue for the Tet holiday. They had previously transported their weapons and ammunition into the city hidden away in wagons, truck beds, and other hiding places. In the early morning hours of January 31, these soldiers retrieved their weapons and took up initial positions within the city, preparing to link up with the NVA and VC assault troops and guide them to their targets.

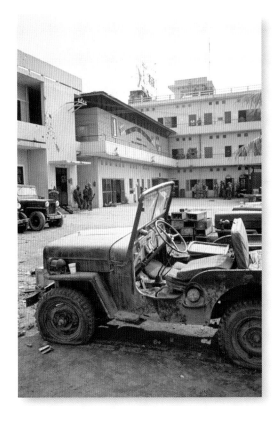

The interior of the MACV Compound in southern Hue City. (Bettmann via Getty Images)

THE INITIAL ATTACK

At 0233hrs on January 31, a signal flare went up in the sky over Hue. North of the river at the Huu Gate in the southwest of the Citadel, a four-man VC sapper team, dressed in ARVN uniforms, killed the guards and opened the gate. The PAVN 6th Regiment, with two battalions of infantry and the 12th Sapper Battalion, poured into the Citadel. The 6th Regiment had three primary objectives—the Mang Ca Compound, the Tay Loc Airfield, and the Imperial Palace.

Once through the gate, the 800th Battalion turned north and attacked toward the airfield, where its advance was initially halted by the Hac Bao company, reinforced by the division's 1st Ordnance Company. Meanwhile, the 802nd Battalion struck east toward the Mang Ca Compound, with the goal of neutralizing the 1st ARVN Division headquarters before Brigadier-General Ngo Quang Truong could rally the city's defenders. At the same time, a company of NVA regulars from the 806th Battalion captured the An Hoa Bridge over the moat at the western tip of the Citadel; sappers then scaled the northwestern wall and, once over the wall, opened a gate to let more of their comrades into the Citadel. The remainder of the 806th Battalion set up a defensive position about a block north of QL 1.

At the Mang Ca Compound, Ngo Quang Truong and his patched-together 200-man defensive force of clerks, doctors, and patients fought back fiercely against the attack by the 802nd Battalion. At one point, the enemy broke

January 31, 1968: Communist attacks

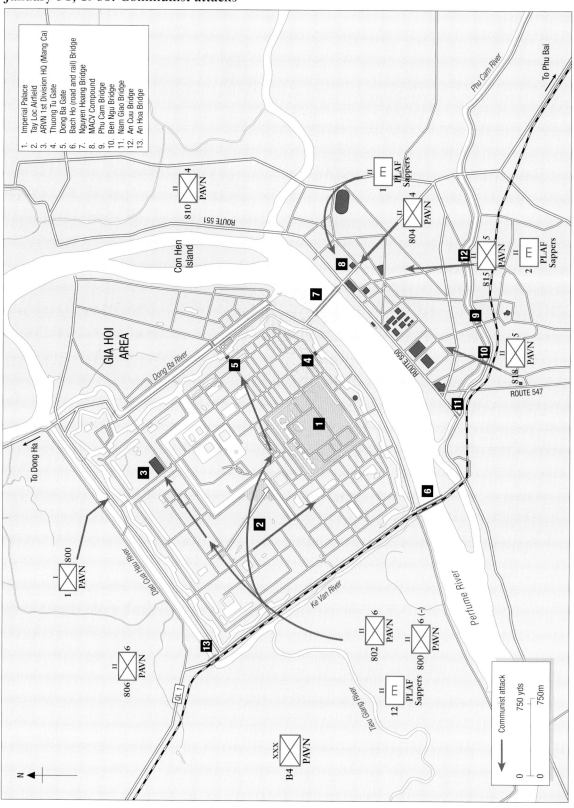

Key:
1. Imperial Palace
2. Tay Loc Airfield
3. ARVN 1st Division HQ (Mang Ca)
4. Thuong Tu Gate
5. Dong Ba Gate
6. Bach Ho (road and rail) Bridge
7. Nguyen Hoang Bridge
8. MACV Compound
9. Phu Cam Bridge
10. Ben Ngu Bridge
11. Nam Giao Bridge
12. An Cuu Bridge
13. An Hoa Bridge

into the medical area, but a staff officer, Lieutenant Nguyen Ai, although wounded in the shoulder, led a counterattack by ARVN clerks and other headquarters personnel that repulsed the NVA attackers.

At the airfield, the outnumbered Black Panther company led by Lieutenant Tran Ngoc Hue, fought desperately against the 800th Battalion, firing M72 LAWs into the attacking enemy ranks and driving them back. Still holding the Mang Ca Compound, but under heavy pressure, Brigadier-General Ngo Quang Truong ordered the Black Panthers to withdraw

A view from a pillbox on the upper levels of the MACV Compound in southern Hue City. The weapon is an M1919 Browning 30-caliber machine gun. (Bettmann via Getty Images)

from the airfield to the compound to help strengthen his position there. When Lieutenant Tran Ngoc Hue and his troops arrived at the compound, Ngo Quang Truong put him in charge of the defenses. In the ensuing battle, the enemy attackers breached the ARVN defenses on several occasions, capturing the hospital and taking the parade field. However, Tran Ngoc Hue personally led counterattacks that repulsed the enemy. Tran Ngoc Hue's US Marine advisor, Captain James J. Cooligan, had nothing but the highest praise for his counterpart, later describing him as "bigger than life in the field."

By daylight on January 31, Brigadier-General Ngo Quang Truong and his men still had a tenuous hold on the compound, but the 6th PAVN Regiment, reinforced by the 12th Sapper Battalion, had overrun the rest of the Citadel, including the Imperial Palace, where the Communists established their command post. Ngo Quang Truong's retention of the Mang Ca Compound would prove key as the battle unfolded; it allowed an access point into the Citadel which could be used by US and South Vietnamese forces rather than having to attack over the walls.

As the 6th PAVN Regiment assaulted the Citadel, Communist gunners launched a 122mm rocket and 82mm mortar barrage from the mountains to the west on both Phu Bai south of the city and Tam Thai on the southeastern edge of the modern city. Following the rocket and mortar barrage, the reinforced 4th PAVN Regiment moved to secure its assigned objectives in the new city on the south bank of the river, which included the MACV Compound, the national police station, the prison, and the Thua Thien Provincial Headquarters. However, rather than launching their attack immediately on the heels of the rocket and mortar barrage, the attackers were disorganized and one unit even lost its way in the darkness, resulting in a five-minute delay between the end of the barrage and the attack on the compound, a complex of two- to three-story buildings. This gave the defenders inside time to grab their weapons and mount a quick defense. Once organized, the 804th PAVN Battalion attacked the northeast corner of the MACV Compound, but the attackers were repelled by the quickly assembled defenders. One US soldier manned an exposed machine-gun position atop a 7m wooden tower; his fire stopped the first rush of North Vietnamese sappers who tried to advance to the compound walls to set satchel charges, but he was killed by a B-40 rocket. The NVA troops then stormed the compound gate, where they were turned back by a group of Marine guards

ATTACK ON THE MACV COMPOUND, JANAURY 31, 1968 (PP. 42–43)

In the early morning hours of January 31, 1968, Viet Cong and North Vietnamese soldiers attacked the city of Hue. The southern wing of the Hue City Front attacked the modern part of the city south of the Perfume River. While other units attacked the Thua Thien Provincial Headquarters, the Treasury, Post Office and other key buildings, elements of the 804th PAVN Battalion and 2nd Sapper Battalion attacked the MACV Compound. Here, Communist troops, armed with an AK-47 (**1**), RPD machine gun (**2**) and B-40 (RPG-2) rocket launcher (**3**) are shown attempting to advance on the MACV compound (**4**), but the advisors inside the street-front building have hurriedly mounted a defense, firing on them from the upper stories with machine guns and rifles.

In the intense two-hour firefight that ensued, the allied advisors repelled the Communist attackers. Failing to take the compound, the Communist troops moved on to easier targets. Meanwhile, the advisors had requested assistance from the Marine headquarters at Phu Bai. Subsequently, two Marine companies were dispatched to the city, attacking up QL 1 (**5**) and reaching the MACV Compound by mid-afternoon. The Marines were subsequently reinforced and ordered to continue the attack to clear the southern sector of Hue City of enemy troops.

manning a bunker. The Communists then tried to make their attack from the southeast corner of the compound, but, after an intense firefight, this attack was repulsed as well. Having failed to take the compound, the Communists tried to reduce it with mortars and automatic weapons fire from overlooking buildings, and then moved on to easier targets. The defenders consolidated their defense and waited for reinforcements.

While the battle raged around the MACV Compound, additional North Vietnamese attackers seized other key buildings, including the police station and other government buildings south of the river. They did not encounter any meaningful resistance except at the Thua Thien Provincial Headquarters, where a platoon of "Hac Boa" soldiers held out until late afternoon. Continuing the attack, the North Vietnamese seized Hue University and the provincial hospital, which they converted into a command post. At the same time, additional NVA troops occupied blocking positions on the southern edge of the city to prevent reinforcement from that direction.

In addition to the 1st ARVN Division headquarters and the MACV Compound, scattered Regional Forces and Popular Forces units continued to hold out, but they were all eventually surrounded and cut off. South Vietnamese troops also managed to retain control of the Navy Boat Ramp on the waterfront to the northeast of the MACV Compound and the 1st Signal Brigade's multichannel rapid relay complex remained in friendly hands; otherwise, however, the North Vietnamese and their VC allies now controlled the city on both sides of the river. This was only too apparent when the sun came up on the morning of January 31; nearly everyone in the city could see the gold-starred, blue-and-red National Liberation Front flag flying high over the Citadel on the Ngo Mon flagpole.

While the PAVN and VC assault troops roamed the streets freely and consolidated their gains, political officers divided the city into areas and put each under the control of a "Revolutionary Committee." All residents were required to report to and register with the Revolutionary Committee in charge of their respective neighborhoods. The residents were ordered to turn in all weapons, ammunition, and radios in their possession. They were then released to return to their homes.

Then began a reign of terror when South Vietnamese and foreigners on the previously prepared special lists of "enemies of the revolution" were rounded up by VC cadre. These "enemies" included government officials, South Vietnamese soldiers, teachers, intellectuals, Catholics, and selected foreigners. VC cadre marched through the Citadel, reading out the names on the lists through loudspeakers and telling those named to report to the local school building. Those that did not report were hunted down. When families inquired as to their condition and the location of their loved ones who had been rounded up, they were told that they were attending a re-education course. However, many of these detainees were never seen again; their fate would not be revealed until sometime after the battle for Hue was concluded.

The National Liberation Front flag was raised over the Citadel on the Ngo Mon flagpole by Communist troops on January 31, 1968; it would fly over the Citadel for 25 days. (Bettman via Getty Images)

As the fighting erupted in Hue, other Communist forces had struck in cities and towns from the DMZ in the north to the tip of the Ca Mau Peninsula in the south, and allied forces had their hands full all over the country. The northern provinces were no exception, where III MAF was focused on the battle for Khe Sanh, but also had to deal with other attacks developing throughout the region. Additionally, US and South Vietnamese forces had been moved to the west to support the action in and around Khe Sanh, thus reducing the number of troops available in the entire northern region. With forces committed all throughout the region, it would prove difficult to assemble sufficient uncommitted combat power to oust the Communists from Hue. This situation would have a major impact on the conduct of subsequent operations to retake Hue from the Communists.

Brigadier-General Ngo Quang Truong, who maintained a tenuous hold on his own headquarters compound, ordered his 3rd Regiment, the 7th Airborne Battalion, and the 7th Armored Cavalry Squadron, back to Hue to reinforce the defenders in the Citadel from their positions outside the city. However, this would prove difficult to accomplish. The North Vietnamese forces had quickly established blocking positions around the city to prevent reinforcements from reaching the beleaguered defenders. The 806th PAVN Battalion blocked QL 1 northwest of Hue, while the 804th PAVN Battalion took up position in southern Hue, establishing a headquarters and a mortar position in the Tu Do Stadium. Additional North Vietnamese soldiers took up positions west of the MACV Compound. At the same time, the 810th PAVN Battalion established a blocking position to the southwest of the city and another NVA company dug in along QL 1 southwest of Hue.

As the South Vietnamese reinforcements neared the Citadel from their respective locations, they encountered well established Communist blocking forces. The 7th Airborne and the 3rd Troop, 7th Armored Cavalry Squadron, made it to about 400m from the Citadel when they were met by withering fire from part of the 806th PAVN Battalion concealed in a cemetery. Two of the cavalry's armored personnel carriers were knocked out.

The paratroopers conducted a frontal assault against the entrenched enemy, but eventually were turned back by intense fire; almost half of the paratroopers were killed or wounded. They called for assistance and Ngo Quang Truong ordered the 2nd Airborne Battalion, in reserve at PK-17, to bypass the enemy roadblocks and move east to approach the Mang Ca Compound from that direction. They attacked the enemy positions in the cemetery from the flank, but were unable to dislodge the NVA pinning down the 7th Battalion. The next morning, the paratroopers found that the enemy had withdrawn into the Citadel. Led by a group of Hac Bao soldiers, they were able to make their way cross-country to the Trit Gate in the Citadel wall near the Mang Ca Compound. Upon arrival of the paratroopers, Ngo Quang Truong ordered the battalion to retake the Tay Loc Airfield.

South of the river, another troop from the 7th Armored Cavalry Squadron, which had pushed forward after making initial contact at the An Cuu Bridge, ran into heavy enemy resistance near the central police station. During this action, the squadron commander, Lieutenant-Colonel Phan Huu Chi, was mortally wounded and four of the unit's armored personnel carriers were knocked out by B-40 rockets.

The 1st and 4th battalions from the 3rd Regiment, which had been operating to the southeast, reached the outskirts of the city from the south.

However, they immediately encountered heavy resistance from the 810th PAVN Battalion in their previously established blocking positions.

The next day, the 1st Battalion soldiers broke contact and marched eastward to Ba Long, a government-controlled outpost on the coast. There they boarded small landing craft and motorized junks for the long trip to the Bao Vinh Pier on the Dao Cua Hau River in Hue. There they offloaded and moved toward the Mang Ca Compound, arriving late in the afternoon of February 1. The 4th Battalion was surrounded and was not able to break out from the encirclement for several days; it would not reach the compound until February 4 and there would only be 170 soldiers left in the unit.

The 2nd and 3rd battalions from the 3rd Regiment were southwest of the city when they got the call from Brigadier-General Ngo Quang Truong. They crossed the Bach Ho road/railroad bridge over the river and made it to the southern corner of the Citadel. Advancing along the bank toward the Ngan Gate, they ran into heavy fire from the entrenched North Vietnamese. Unable to advance through the gate, a squad of ARVN soldiers attempted to climb over the wall with ladders. They made it over the wall, but were all were immediately killed by a flurry of enemy fire. Unable to breach the Citadel wall, the ARVN established night defensive positions just outside the southeast wall and awaited new orders. They were subsequently ordered to clear the enemy forces in the residential area between the Citadel and the Perfume River, resulting in a brutal two-day house-to-house fight in which the ARVN casualties piled up and which left the NVA still in control of the area. Ngo Quang Truong committed another battalion to the battle and the attack against the entrenched NVA defenders continued, but in the costly fighting that ensued, the ARVN were unsuccessful in breaching the enemy's interlocking defenses.

As Brigadier-General Ngo Quang Truong and his forces attempted to carry the attack to the enemy, a call for reinforcements went out from the surrounded MACV Compound. This plea for assistance was almost lost in all the confusion caused by the simultaneous attacks going on all over I CTZ. Neither Lieutenant-General Hoang Xuan Lam at I Corps headquarters, nor Lieutenant-General Cushman at III MAF, were sure what exactly was happening inside Hue. The enemy strength and the scope of the Communist attack was less than clear during the early hours of the battle, but the allied commanders realized that reinforcements would be needed to eject the Communists from the city. Accordingly, Cushman ordered TF X-Ray to send reinforcements into Hue to relieve the besieged MACV Compound.

While both ARVN and US commanders tried to assess the situation and made preparations to move reinforcements to Hue, the NVA attacked and overran the municipal prison south of the river, freeing approximately 2,000 prisoners that were incarcerated there. After being freed, a large proportion of the prisoners were pressed into service as laborers while others were given weapons and joined combat units as replacements.

THE MARINES RESPOND

Responding to III MAF orders, Brigadier-General LaHue, commander of TF X-Ray, directed A/1/1st Marines, commanded by Captain Gordon D. Batcheller, to move up QL 1 from Phu Bai by truck to relieve the surrounded

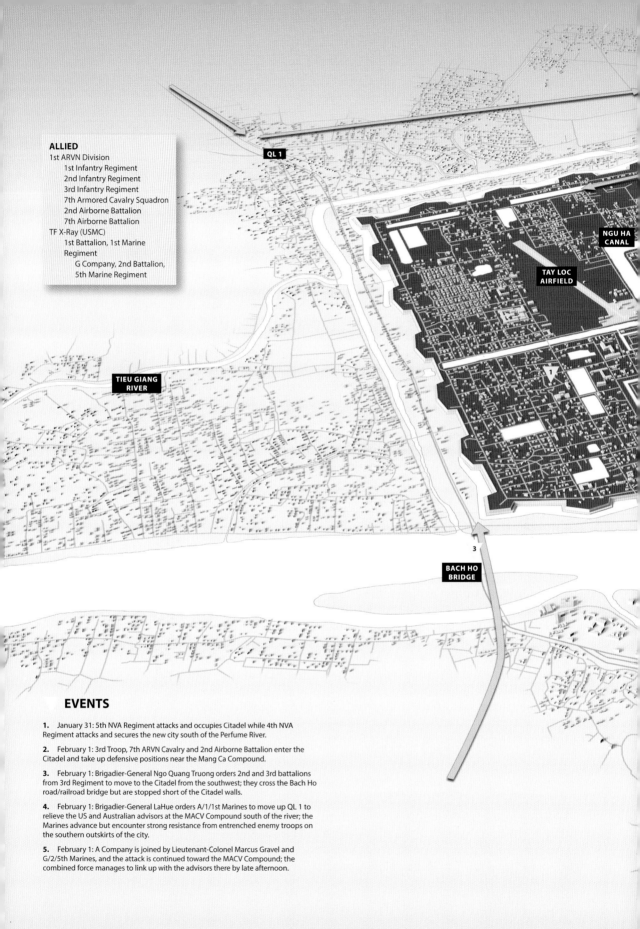

ALLIED
1st ARVN Division
   1st Infantry Regiment
   2nd Infantry Regiment
   3rd Infantry Regiment
   7th Armored Cavalry Squadron
   2nd Airborne Battalion
   7th Airborne Battalion
TF X-Ray (USMC)
   1st Battalion, 1st Marine
   Regiment
      G Company, 2nd Battalion,
      5th Marine Regiment

QL 1

NGU HA CANAL

TAY LOC AIRFIELD

TIEU GIANG RIVER

BACH HO BRIDGE

EVENTS

1. January 31: 5th NVA Regiment attacks and occupies Citadel while 4th NVA Regiment attacks and secures the new city south of the Perfume River.

2. February 1: 3rd Troop, 7th ARVN Cavalry and 2nd Airborne Battalion enter the Citadel and take up defensive positions near the Mang Ca Compound.

3. February 1: Brigadier-General Ngo Quang Truong orders 2nd and 3rd battalions from 3rd Regiment to move to the Citadel from the southwest; they cross the Bach Ho road/railroad bridge but are stopped short of the Citadel walls.

4. February 1: Brigadier-General LaHue orders A/1/1st Marines to move up QL 1 to relieve the US and Australian advisors at the MACV Compound south of the river; the Marines advance but encounter strong resistance from entrenched enemy troops on the southern outskirts of the city.

5. February 1: A Company is joined by Lieutenant-Colonel Marcus Gravel and G/2/5th Marines, and the attack is continued toward the MACV Compound; the combined force manages to link up with the advisors there by late afternoon.

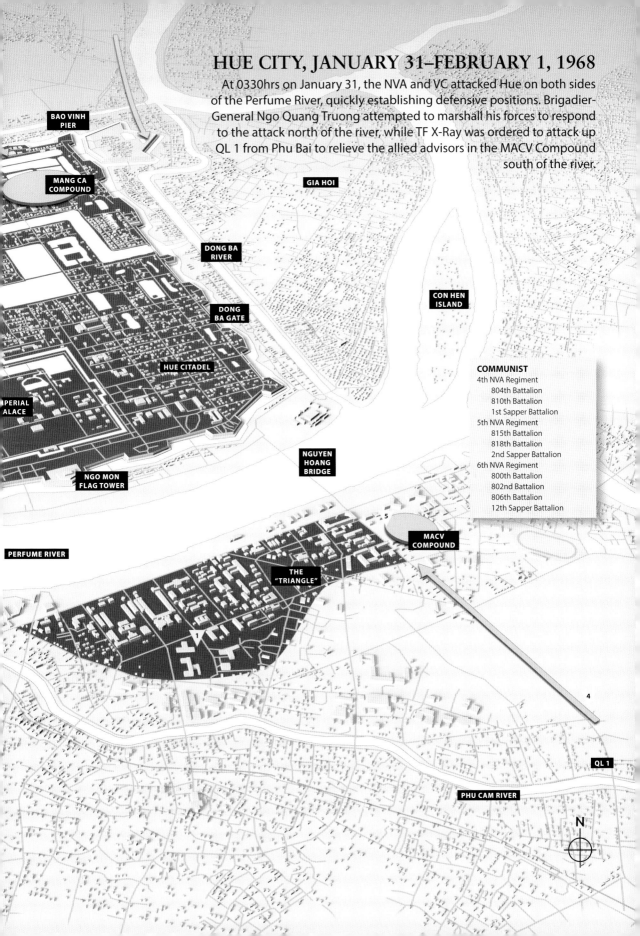

HUE CITY, JANUARY 31–FEBRUARY 1, 1968

At 0330hrs on January 31, the NVA and VC attacked Hue on both sides of the Perfume River, quickly establishing defensive positions. Brigadier-General Ngo Quang Truong attempted to marshall his forces to respond to the attack north of the river, while TF X-Ray was ordered to attack up QL 1 from Phu Bai to relieve the allied advisors in the MACV Compound south of the river.

BAO VINH PIER

MANG CA COMPOUND

GIA HOI

DONG BA RIVER

DONG BA GATE

CON HEN ISLAND

HUE CITADEL

IPERIAL ALACE

NGO MON FLAG TOWER

NGUYEN HOANG BRIDGE

COMMUNIST
4th NVA Regiment
  804th Battalion
  810th Battalion
  1st Sapper Battalion
5th NVA Regiment
  815th Battalion
  818th Battalion
  2nd Sapper Battalion
6th NVA Regiment
  800th Battalion
  802nd Battalion
  806th Battalion
  12th Sapper Battalion

MACV COMPOUND

PERFUME RIVER

THE "TRIANGLE"

QL 1

PHU CAM RIVER

N

US advisors at the MACV Compound. The initial report of the attack on Ngo Quang Truong's headquarters and the subsequent request from the MACV advisors had not caused any great alarm at the task force headquarters. LaHue, having received no reliable intelligence to the contrary, believed that only a small enemy force had penetrated Hue as part of a local diversionary attack; little did he know that almost a full enemy division had seized the city. At the same time, all of his outposts from the Hai Van Pass to Phu Bai were under attack and many of the roads connecting them were impassable because of ambushes or mines. With little else to spare, LaHue therefore sent only one company to deal with the situation in Hue.

Not knowing exactly what to expect when they reached the city, the Marines from A/1/1st Marines, along with two M55 US Army gun trucks armed with quad .50-caliber machine guns, headed north as ordered, joining up with four Marine M48A3 tanks from the 3rd Tank Battalion en route. The column ran into sniper fire and had to stop several times to clear buildings along the route of march. When the lead vehicles approached the An Cuu Bridge over the Phu Cam River, they encountered the wrecked South Vietnamese armored personnel carriers from the 7th Cavalry Squadron. Upon crossing the bridge, the Marines were immediately caught in a withering crossfire from enemy automatic weapons, B-40 rockets, and 75mm recoilless rifle fire that seemed to come from every direction; a direct hit by one rocket killed the tank commander in the lead tank. As the Marines and the accompanying tanks advanced slowly against intense enemy resistance, they became pinned down between the Perfume and Phu Cam rivers, just short of the MACV Compound they had been sent to relieve.

At one point during the fighting, Marine Sergeant Alfredo Gonzalez single-handedly took out an enemy bunker, permitting his comrades to inch forward slowly. During the fight, the company commander, Captain Batcheller, was wounded, as were a number of his Marines. Gunnery Sergeant J. L. Caney took command of the company as the intense fighting continued; Caney would receive a much belated Medal of Honor in 2018 for his actions in the battle for Hue.

With A Company pinned down, Lieutenant-Colonel Marcus J. Gravel, the battalion commander of 1/1st Marines, organized a hasty reaction force, which included himself, his operations officer, several others from his battalion command group (to include the battalion chaplain, Lieutenant Richard Lyons, US Navy), and G/2/5th Marines, a unit from another battalion that had just arrived in Phu Bai earlier that day. Gravel had never met Captain Charles L. Meadows, the G Company commander, until that day, and he later said that the only planning he had time to accomplish was to issue the order: "Get on the trucks, men."

With little information other than that their fellow Marines were pinned down, the relief force moved up the highway, reinforced with two self-propelled M42 twin-40mm guns. The force met little resistance along the way until it crossed the An Cuu Bridge and linked up with A/1/1st Marines, which had taken up defensive positions along the road. With the aid of the four tanks and the 40mm self-propelled guns, the combined force pushed forward under fire toward the MACV Compound, breaking through to the beleaguered defenders at about 1515hrs. The cost, however, was high: ten Marines were killed and 30 were wounded.

At the MACV Compound, Gravel met with Colonel George O. Atkisson, the US Army senior advisor to the 1st ARVN Division, who told him that the "Citadel was in fine shape." This contradicted information that General LaHue back in Phu Bai had received that indicated the 1st ARVN Division was "in trouble" across the river. Accordingly, LaHue directed Gravel to cross the Perfume River with his battalion and break through to relieve the 1st ARVN Division headquarters in the Mang Ca Compound. Gravel protested that his "battalion" consisted of only two companies, one of which was in pretty bad shape, and that part of his force would have to be left behind to assist with the defense of the MACV Compound. Nevertheless, LaHue, who still had not realized the full extent of the enemy's strength in Hue, radioed back that Gravel was to "go anyway." Sending Gravel's battered force to contend with the much stronger PAVN and VC north of the river would ultimately prove problematic.

Leaving A Company behind to help with the defense of the MACV Compound, Gravel ordered Captain Meadows and G Company to move out toward the Nguyen Hoang Bridge near the Navy Boat Ramp. Reinforced with three of the original M48 tanks and several M41 tanks from the ARVN 7th Armored Cavalry Squadron, G Company approached the bridge. However, the bridge was not strong enough to support the weight of the M48A3 tanks. It would support the lighter ARVN tanks, but the South Vietnamese crews, having already lost several vehicles to enemy rocket-propelled grenades, refused to cross the bridge.

Leaving the tanks on the southern bank to support by fire, Captain Meadows and his men attempted to cross the river. As two platoons of infantry started across the bridge, they were met with a hail of fire from a machine-gun nest and recoilless rifles positioned at the north end of the bridge. Ten Marines went down. Lance Corporal Lester A. Tully, who later received the Silver Star for his action, rushed forward and took out the machine gun with a grenade. The two platoons followed Tully, made it over the bridge, and turned left, paralleling the Perfume River along the Citadel's southeast wall. They immediately came under heavy fire from AK-47 rifles, machine guns, B-40 rockets, and recoilless rifles from the walls of the Citadel.

As mortar shells and rockets exploded around them, the Marines tried to push forward, but were pinned down by the increasing volume of enemy fire. Gravel determined that his force was greatly outnumbered and decided to withdraw. However, even that proved very difficult. According to Gravel, the enemy was well dug-in and "firing from virtually every building in Hue city" north of the river. Gravel called for vehicle support to assist in evacuating his wounded, but nothing was available. Eventually, the Marines commandeered some abandoned Vietnamese civilian vehicles and used them as makeshift ambulances. After two hours of intense fighting, the Marines were able to pull back to the bridge and cross back over the river to the south side, carrying their dead and wounded.

By 2000hrs, the 1st Battalion had established a defensive position near the MACV Compound along a stretch of

A US Marine armed with an M16A1 rifle takes cover behind a destroyed vehicle in southern Hue, Vietnam, February 3, 1968. An M48 tank can be seen in the background. (Bettmann via Getty Images)

riverbank that included a park and the Navy Boat Ramp, which the Marines transformed into a helicopter landing site in order to facilitate resupply and evacuate the most seriously wounded.

The attempt by the Marines to force their way across the bridge had been costly. Among the casualties were Chaplain Lyons and Major Walter D. Murphy, the S-3 Operations Officer of the 1st Battalion, who later died from his wounds. Captain Meadows, commander of G Company, lost one-third of his unit killed or wounded "going across that one bridge and then getting back across the bridge." In total, the two Marine companies suffered ten Marines killed and 56 wounded on the first day of the battle.

Despite detailed reports from Lieutenant-Colonel Gravel, Brigadier-General LaHue and his intelligence officers still did not have a good appreciation of what was happening in Hue. Nevertheless, LaHue told a United Press International reporter on the second day of fighting, "Very definitely, we control the South side of the city." However, he later explained, "Early intelligence did not reveal the quantity of enemy involved that we subsequently found were committed to Hue."

The intelligence picture in Saigon was just as confused; General Westmoreland cabled General Earle Wheeler, Chairman of the Joint Chiefs, that the "enemy has approximately three companies in the Hue Citadel and Marines have sent a battalion into the area to clear them out." Subsequent MACV press releases emphasized that the enemy was being "mopped up." At the time, there were over 6,000 PAVN and VC troops occupying Hue. The repeated gross underestimation of enemy strength in Hue initially resulted in insufficient forces being allocated for retaking the city.

With Brigadier-General Ngo Quang Truong and the 1st ARVN Division fully occupied in the Citadel north of the river, Lieutenant-General Hoang Xuan Lam and General Cushman discussed how to divide responsibility for the effort to retake Hue. They eventually agreed that ARVN would be responsible for clearing Communist forces from the Citadel and the rest of Hue north of the river, while TF X-Ray would assume responsibility for the southern part of the city south of the river. This situation resulted in what would be, initially, two separate and distinct battles that would rage in Hue, one south of the river and one north of the river. At the same time, Cushman received permission from MACV to use the 1st Cavalry Division to pressure the Communists from the west while the Marines and South Vietnamese forces continued the fight for the city.

In retaking Hue, Hoang Xuan Lam and Cushman were confronted with a unique problem. The ancient capital was almost sacred to the Vietnamese people, particularly so to the Buddhists. The destruction of the city would result in political repercussions that neither the United States nor the government of South Vietnam could afford. Cushman later recalled, "I wasn't about to open up on the old palace and all the historical buildings there." As a result, limitations were imposed on the use of artillery and close air support to minimize collateral damage. Eventually these restrictions would be lifted when it was realized that both artillery and close air support would be necessary to dislodge the enemy from the city. However, the initial rules of engagement played a key role in the difficulties incurred in the early days of the battle.

Having divided up the city, Cushman began to make arrangements to send more reinforcements into the Hue area in an attempt to seal off the enemy inside the city from outside support. On February 1, he alerted the US Army 1st Cavalry Division under Major-General John J. Tolson to be prepared to deploy his 3rd Brigade into a sector west of the city, with the mission of blocking the enemy approaches into Hue from the north and west.

On February 2, the 3rd Brigade commander, Colonel Hubert S. Campbell, ordered his 2nd Battalion, 12th Cavalry (2/12th Cavalry) to move by helicopter from Camp Evans where it had been carrying out base defense missions into a landing zone near PK-17, about 10km northwest of Hue on QL 1. Its mission was to move toward Hue, make contact with the enemy, and establish a blocking position to attempt to preclude enemy reinforcement of the city from that direction. The 2/12th Cavalry commander, Lieutenant-Colonel Richard S. Sweet, ordered his battalion to avoid the enemy troops along QL 1 by first moving south before turning to the east toward Hue.

A wounded US Marine is helped out of the fighting area by a couple of buddies as Communist snipers continue to inflict casualties on allied soldiers. (Bettman via Getty Images)

By February 5, the cavalry troopers had been inserted into the LZ and began moving cross-country. With the aid of artillery and helicopter gunships, they fought through heavy enemy resistance at the hamlet of Thon Que Chu, sustaining nine killed and another 48 wounded. The enemy counterattacked and 2/12th Cavalry soon found itself in heavy contact. The cavalry troopers managed to establish a defensive position on a hill named Nha Nhan, which overlooked a valley about 6km west of Hue. From there, the unit directed artillery and naval gunfire against the enemy below in an attempt to keep the enemy from moving reinforcement and supplies into Hue.

During the same period, the 5th Battalion, 7th Cavalry (5/7th Cavalry) conducted search and clear operations along enemy routes south of Camp Evans. On February 7, it made contact with an entrenched North Vietnamese force near the hamlets of Thon Trung and Thon Lieu Coc Tuong. It tried for the next 24 hours to expel the Communists, but the enemy held their position and stymied the cavalry advance with heavy volumes of automatic weapons and mortar fire.

On February 9, 3rd Brigade ordered 5/7th Cavalry to fix the PAVN in place, while directing 2/12th Cavalry to attack northward from its position. The latter ran into heavy resistance near the hamlet of Thon Bon Tri, but continued to fight its way toward 5/7th Cavalry's position. For the next ten days, the two cavalry battalions fought with the entrenched communists, who held their positions against repeated assaults. Despite the inability of the cavalry troopers to expel the North Vietnamese, this action at least partially blocked the enemy's movement and inhibited their participation in the battle raging in Hue.

FIGHTING SOUTH OF THE PERFUME RIVER CONTINUES

As allied reinforcements began their movement to the area, the ARVN and Marines began making preparations for counterattacks in their assigned areas. Making their tasks more difficult was the weather, which took a turn for the worse on February 2, when the temperature fell into the 50s°F and the low clouds opened up with a steady cold drenching rain, making flight operations difficult if not impossible.

As rain fell, Lieutenant-Colonel Gravel's "bobtailed" 1/1st Marines, was ordered to attack to seize the Thua Thien Provincial Headquarters building and prison, a distance of six blocks west of the MACV Compound. At 0700hrs, Gravel launched a two-company attack supported by tanks to take his assigned objectives, but the Marines immediately ran into the 815th PAVN Battalion, which was in prepared fighting positions blocking the Marine advance. An M79 gunner from G Company recalled, "We didn't get a block away [from the MACV compound] when we started getting sniper fire. We got a tank … went a block, turned right and received 57mm recoilless which put out our tank." The attack was "stopped cold" and the battalion fell back to its original position near the MACV Compound.

By this time, Brigadier-General LaHue had finally realized that he and his intelligence officers had vastly underestimated the strength of the Communists south of the river. Accordingly, he called in Colonel Stanley S. Hughes, new commander of the 1st Marine Regiment, and gave him overall tactical control of US forces in the southern part of the city. Assuming control of the battle, Hughes promised Gravel reinforcements and gave him the general mission to conduct "sweep and clear operations … to destroy enemy forces, protect US Nationals and restore that [southern] portion of the city to US control."

In response to Hughes' orders, Gravel directed F/2/5th Marines, which had been placed under his operational control the previous day, to relieve the MACV communications facility near the US consulate, which was surrounded by a VC force, and to clear several Hue University buildings a block to the north. Arriving by Marine CH-46 helicopters at the soccer field near the Navy Boat Ramp at 1500hrs, the company, commanded by Captain Michael P. Downs, launched the attack as ordered. Fighting most of the afternoon, it failed to reach the US Army signal troops, losing three Marines killed and 13 wounded in the process. Downs later remembered that nothing he had been told at Phu Bai prepared him for the situation his company confronted when it arrived in Hue.

Lieutenant-Colonel Gravel wanted to renew the attack and called for air support to suppress the enemy positions, but the low ceiling that had settled in precluded flying. At that point, Gravel's troops established night defensive positions and prepared to continue the attack next morning.

Supported by tanks, US Marines move to clear buildings in street fighting near Hue University. (USMC/DOD)

The next day, the Marines made some headway and brought in further reinforcements. The 1st Battalion relieved the 1st Signals radio facility in the late morning hours and after an intense three-hour fight, reached the university campus. During the night, Communist sappers had dropped the Bach Ho road/railroad bridge across the Perfume River southwest of the city, but a sapper attack to destroy the An Cuu Bridge across the Phu Cam River had failed and, inexplicably, the bridge was still standing.

At 1100hrs on February 2, H/2/5th Marines, commanded by Captain G. Ronald Christmas, crossed the bridge over the Phu Cam River in a convoy, accompanied by Army trucks equipped with quad .50-caliber machine guns and two M50 Ontos (tracked vehicles armed with six 106mm recoilless rifles). As the convoy neared the MACV Compound, it came under intense enemy heavy machine-gun and rocket fire. The Marines responded rapidly, and in the ensuing confusion, the convoy exchanged fire with another Marine unit already in the city. As one Marine in the convoy remembered, "our guys happened to be out on the right side of the road and of course nobody knew that. First thing you know everybody began shooting at our own men ... out of pure fright and frenzy." Luckily, neither of the Marine units took any casualties.

Marines from A/1/1st Marines lower a wounded comrade from a rooftop of the university during the battle for Hue south of the river. (USMC/DOD)

H Company joined Lieutenant-Colonel Gravel where the 1st Battalion had established a position near the MACV Compound. The PAVN and VC gunners continued to pour machine-gun and rocket fire into the position, and by day's end, the Marines at that location had sustained two dead and 34 wounded.

On February 3, Colonel Hughes decided to move his command group into Hue, where he could more directly control the battle. Accompanying Hughes in the convoy that departed for the city was Lieutenant-Colonel Ernest C. Cheatham, Jr, commander of 2/5th Marines, who had been sitting frustrated in Phu Bai while three of his units—F, G, and H companies—fought in Hue under Lieutenant-Colonel Gravel's control. Cheatham, known as "big Ernie" to his friends, had played professional football during the 1950s as a defensive tackle with the Pittsburg Steelers and Baltimore Colts. With only the briefest of orders, Cheatham prepared to join the fight; he later observed, "We went in blind."

Hughes and his command group moved up the highway from Phu Bai by armed convoy. They took enemy fire as they crossed the Phu Cam River, but kept pushing forward, arriving at the MACV Compound around 1300hrs. Hughes quickly established his command post in the officers' club. The forces at his disposal included Cheatham's three companies from 2/5th Marines, which had reverted to Cheatham's control upon his arrival in Hue, and Gravel's depleted battalion consisting of A/1/1st Marines and a provisional company consisting of one platoon of B/1/1st Marines, and several dozen cooks and clerks who had been sent to the front lines to fight.

Hughes wasted no time in taking control of the situation, marshalling his forces and at the same time directing the establishment of a Forward

During the fighting south of the river, CBS News correspondent John Laurence interviews Lieutenant-Colonel Ernest C. Cheatham, Jr, USMC, commander of 2/5th Marines. (CBS via Getty Images)

Logistical Support Area just south of the Nguyen Tri Phuong School. His orders from General LaHue had been succinct: he was to clear the modern city on the south side of the river, while Brigadier-General Ngo Quang Truong and his South Vietnamese troops focused on clearing the Citadel. With his logistics support in place, Hughes quickly devised a plan. He directed Gravel to anchor the left flank with his one-and-a-half-company battalion to keep QL 1, the main supply route, open. Then he ordered Cheatham and his three companies to assume responsibility for the attack southwest from Hue University along Route 550 (Le Loi Street) toward the Provincial Headquarters, paralleling the river. He told Cheatham to "attack through the city and clean the NVA out." When Cheatham hesitated, waiting for additional guidance, the regimental commander who, like everyone else going into Hue, had only the sketchiest information, gruffly stated, "if you're looking for any more, you aren't going to get it. Move out!" He added, "You do it any way you want, and you get any heat from above, I'll take care of that."

Cheatham came up with a plan that called for his battalion to move west along the river from the MACV Compound. He would attack with companies F and H in the lead and G Company in reserve; H Company would capture the public health building and F Company, the Post Office and Treasury buildings. Although the plan was simple, execution proved extremely difficult. From the MACV compound southwestward to the confluence of the Perfume River and the Phu Cam River was almost 11 blocks, each of which had been transformed by the enemy into a fortress that would have to be cleared building by building, room by room. It would prove to be a brutal affair.

US Marines at a forward command post as the allied attack continues to clear the south bank of the Perfume River of Communist troops. (Terry Fincher/Daily Express/ Hulton Archive/Getty Images)

This kind of fighting was new to the Marines; US forces had not fought in urban terrain since the battle for Seoul in September 1950 and most of the Marines were too young to have served in Korea. They were accustomed to fighting an enemy in sparsely populated jungles or open terrain away from built-up areas of any significance. Fighting in such close quarters against an entrenched enemy was decidedly different from what the Marines had been trained to do.

Like most South Vietnamese cities, the streets were narrow and most of the houses and other structures were separated by high walls or hedgerows, which were usually topped with barbed-wire; additionally, the stone and masonry walls often had broken glass or other sharp objects imbedded along their tops. Many of the homes had their own foxholes and bunkers constructed by the residents for their own protection. Thus, each house became a separate defensive position and each block a formidable bastion.

From a classroom in Hue University, a Marine fires his M16 rifle at a sniper as his fellow Marines advance against the entrenched Communist troops south of the Perfume River. (USMC/DOD)

With no training in this kind of environment, the Marines essentially had to develop their own tactics, techniques, and procedures as they went along. The first three days of the battle had been a bloody learning process as the Marines went through what was in effect live-fire on-the-job training in house-to-house fighting. The tactics that they had used so effectively in previous operations in I CTZ in less built-up areas had little application inside the city. The Marines had to devise ways to defeat the entrenched enemy who used the myriad of buildings, walls, and towers so effectively; they would have to learn by trial and error.

Cheatham's Marines began their attack toward the Treasury building and Post Office, but they made very slow progress, not having yet devised workable tactics to deal with the demands of the urban terrain. As the Marines, supported by tanks, tried to advance, the Communists hit them with a withering array of mortar, rocket, machine-gun, and small-arms fire from prepared positions in the buildings. According to Cheatham, his Marines tried to take the Treasury and Post Office five or six different times. He later recalled, "You'd assault and back you'd come, drag your wounded and then muster [the energy and courage] up again and try it again."

The Marines did not have enough men to deal with the enemy entrenched in the buildings. The frontage for a company was about one block, and with two companies forward, this left an exposed left flank, subject to enemy automatic weapons and rocket fire. By the evening of February 3, the Marines had made little progress and were taking increasing casualties as they fought back and forth over the same ground.

The following morning, Colonel Hughes met with his two battalion commanders. He directed Cheatham to continue the attack. He told Gravel to continue to secure Cheatham's left flank with his battalion, which now had only one company, A Company, commanded by First Lieutenant Ray L. Smith, who had taken over for the wounded Captain Batcheller. As Gravel ordered Smith's company into position to screen Cheatham's attack, the

TF X-RAY MARINES FIGHT THEIR WAY THROUGH SOUTHERN HUE, FEBRUARY 8–9, 1968 (PP. 58–59)

Once the Marines from TF X-Ray had fought their way to the MACV Compound southeast of the Nguyen Hoang Bridge over the Perfume River and linked up with the advisors there, they made an unsuccessful attempt to cross the bridge over the Perfume River into the Citadel. The Marines were then reinforced and ordered to attack southwest along the river from the MACV Compound to the confluence of the Perfume and Phu Cam rivers, some 11 blocks away, clearing the area of Communist troops.

As the Marines launched their attack, supported by tanks and M-50 Ontos, they immediately came under intense fire. The battle quickly degenerated into a brutal room-to-room, house-to-house fight. Advancing with determination against the entrenched Communist fighters, the two Marine battalions steadily retook the Thua Thien Provincial Headquarters, Hue University, and other key buildings on the south side, reaching

their objectives at the confluence of the river and the canal on February 11.

Shown here is a typical scene from the fighting on the south side of Hue City, where the Marines (**1**) fought their way through the shattered remains of houses and gardens (**2**), clearing them with whatever supporting fire was available, blowing holes in walls with recoilless rifles, then sending fire teams and squads into the breach. Taking advantage of Hue's numerous courtyards and walled estates, the NVA and VC fought the Marines every step of the way. The Marines were particularly enthusiastic about the M-50 Ontos (**3**), which was used very effectively in the direct-fire mode to suppress enemy positions and to blow holes in the buildings so the Marines could advance.

Among the personal weapons carried by the Marines shown here are the 5.56mm M16 rifle (**4**), and the 40mm M79 grenade launcher (**5**)

A CH-46 helicopter prepares to evacuate wounded Marines at the allied landing zone on the south bank of the Perfume River. (Bettman via Getty Images)

Marines first had to secure the Joan of Arc School and Church (known today as St Francis Xavier Catholic Church). They immediately ran into heavy contact with the enemy and were forced to fight house-to-house. During the fighting, Sergeant Alfredo Gonzalez, who had performed so valiantly the first day of the battle, took out one enemy position, but a B-40 rocket struck him in the stomach, killing him instantly. For this action and his earlier heroism, Gonzalez would be posthumously awarded the Medal of Honor.

Eventually the Marines secured the school, but continued to take effective fire from NVA and VC gunners in the church. Gravel later recalled, "[The enemy soldiers] were up in the eaves, the wooden overhead; and they were in there and we couldn't get them out." Reluctantly, Gravel gave the order to fire upon the church and the Marines pounded the building with mortars and 106mm recoilless rifle fire, eventually killing or driving off the enemy. In the ruins of the church, the Marines found two European priests, one French and one Belgian, who were livid that the Marines had fired on the church. Gravel was sorry for the destruction, but felt that he had had no choice in the matter.

With Gravel's Marines moving into position to screen his left flank on the Phu Cam River, Cheatham launched his attack at 0700hrs on February 4. Captain Christmas and H Company would seize the public health building in front of the university where it could provide supporting fires from the flank as Captain Downs and F Company assaulted the Treasury and Post Office complex across from Hue University.

Captain Christmas later remembered his apprehension as his unit prepared to enter the battle for Hue: "I could feel a knot developing in my stomach. Not so much from fear—though a helluva lot of fear was there—but because we were new

Two US Marines climb the stairs of a severely bullet-pocked building south of the Perfume River. (Bettman via Getty Images)

The ruins of St Francis Xavier Catholic Church (referred to as "Joan of Arc Church" in US sources on the battle), located at 18 Nguyen Tri Phuong Street in southern Hue. It was heavily damaged by enemy and US fire missions, and was the scene of a bloody battle for control of the building. (USMC/DOD)

to this type of situation. We were accustomed to jungles and open rice fields, and now we would be fighting in a city, like it was Europe during World War II. One of the beautiful things about the Marines is that they adapt quickly, but we were going to take a number of casualties learning some basic lessons in this experience."

The Marines launched their attack as ordered, supported by 90mm tank fire, 106mm recoilless rifles, and 81mm mortars. In the rapidly deteriorating weather, they found themselves in a room-by-room, building-by-building struggle to clear an eleven-by-nine block area just south of the river. This effort rapidly turned into a bloody slugfest as the Marines advanced under heavy enemy fire.

Blasting its way through walls and courtyards with 3.5-inch rockets, Captain Christmas' company took the public health building. Having taken the building, H Company was then able to support F Company's assault on the Treasury. After repeated efforts to force its way into the building, F Company resorted to the use of CS gas against the enemy. Using E-8 tear gas launchers, the Marines, wearing gas masks, renewed their attack supported by 81mm mortars and fire from 3.5-inch rocket launchers. Once the Marines breached the building, the NVA, according to Captain Downs, "exited the building as quickly as they could" to escape the Marine advance.

The fight for the city south of the river was savage work—house-to-house fighting through city streets. Ground gained in the fighting was to be measured in centimetres and each city block cost dearly, as every alley, street corner, window and garden had to be paid for in blood. Correspondents who moved forward with the Marines reported the fighting as the most intense they had ever seen in South Vietnam.

The combat was relentless. Small groups of Marines moved doggedly from house to house, assaulting enemy positions with whatever supporting fire was available, blowing holes in walls with rocket launchers or recoilless rifles, then sending fire teams and squads into the breach. Each structure had to be cleared room by room using M16 rifles and grenades. Taking advantage of Hue's numerous courtyards and walled estates, the NVA and VC fought the Marines every step of the way.

One of the practical problems that the Marines encountered early was the lack of sufficiently detailed maps. Originally their only references were standard 1:50,000-scale tactical maps that showed little of the city detail. One company commander later remarked, "You have to raid the local Texaco station to get your street map. That's really what you need." Eventually, Cheatham and Gravel got the necessary maps and numbered the government and municipal buildings and prominent city features. This permitted them to coordinate their efforts more closely.

Making the problem of clearing the area even more difficult was the initial prohibition on using artillery and close air support. The Marines had a vast arsenal of heavy weapons at their disposal: 105mm, 155mm, and 8-inch howitzers, helicopter gunships, close air support from fighter-bombers, and naval gunfire from destroyers and cruisers with 5-inch, 6-inch, and 8-inch guns standing just offshore. However, because of the initial rules of engagement that sought to limit damage to the city, these resources were not authorized for use by the Marines at the beginning of the battle.

Even after Lieutenant-General Hoang Xuan Lam lifted the ban on the use of fire support south of the river on February 3, the Marines could not depend on air support or artillery because of the close quarters and the low-lying cloud cover. Lieutenant-Colonel Gravel later explained part of the difficulty: "Artillery in an area like that is not terribly effective because you can't observe it well enough. You lose the rounds in the buildings in the street … and you have a difficult time with perspective." Additionally, the poor weather, which also greatly limited close air support, had a negative impact on the utility of artillery because the rounds had to be adjusted by sound when the flashes were swallowed by the low clouds and fog.

Luckily, the Marines had other firepower at their disposal. They used tanks to support their advance, but found they were unwieldy in close quarters and drew antitank fire nearly every time they advanced. Lieutenant-Colonel Cheatham later recalled: "The moment a tank stuck its nose around the corner of a building, it looked like the Fourth of July." According to Cheatham, one tank took over 120 hits from B-40 antitank rockets.

The Marines were much more enthusiastic about the M50 Ontos, which were used very effectively in the direct fire mode to suppress enemy positions and to blow holes in the buildings so the Marines could advance. Despite their preference for the Ontos, the Marines made use of every weapon at their disposal in order to dislodge the NVA and VC troops, to include 3.5-inch rockets and mortars. The rockets, which could penetrate 28cm of steel, were used to great effect in breaching walls, while the Marines dropped mortar rounds on top of buildings like "sledge hammers."

In the early evening hours of February 4, a sapper platoon finally managed to destroy the An Cuu Bridge over the Phu Cam River, severing the ground link between Hue and Phu Bai. Until the span was repaired, the Americans in southern Hue would have to rely on helicopters and rivercraft for all their logistical needs. However, continuing bad weather and enemy gunners made resupply by air increasingly difficult.

Gas mask-clad Marines of 2/5th Marines move in to clear the Treasury building. (USMC/DOD)

The fighting continued without let-up; progress was deliberate, methodical, and costly. Lieutenant-Colonel Gravel later recalled, "The going was slow … We fought for two days over one building." Nevertheless, the Marines continued the advance. On the right flank, Captain Christmas' H/2/5th Marines advanced southwestward along Route 550, paralleling the Perfume River front. The two companies from the 1st Battalion advanced on the left flank. Their next objectives were the Hospital and the Thua Thien Provincial Headquarters, a large, two-story L-shaped building surrounded by a 2.4m-high wall.

As the Marines neared the wall, they came under heavy enemy fire. Using two

Two US Marines help a third to walk through a destroyed gateway entrance to Hue Hospital, where they will seek medical aid for their wounded comrade. (Bettman via Getty Images)

tanks and 106mm recoilless rifles mounted on Mechanical Mules (a flat-bedded, self-propelled carrier about the size of a jeep), the Marines advanced against intense automatic-weapons fire, rockets, and mortars. Responding with an M48A3 tank, 106mm recoilless rifles, and their own mortars and CS gas, the Marines from Captain Meadow's G Company finally overwhelmed the defenders in the main hospital building around 1630hrs.

The following morning, the Marines continued their attack, clearing the hospital complex with three companies on line. By late afternoon, F Company had cleared the last of the hospital buildings, sustaining four killed and 11 wounded in the course of the battle.

Meanwhile, Captain Meadows' G Company attacked the provincial prison. The Marines blasted holes in the prison walls and fired CS cannisters into the building. Wearing gas masks, the Marines surged forward, killing 36 NVA and securing the building.

On the battalion's right flank, the Marines from Captain Christmas' H Company began its assault on the Provincial Headquarters at 0950hrs. Supported by two M48A3 tanks and a tripod-mounted 106mm recoilless rifle, the Marines donned gas masks and launched their attack under cover of CS gas. However, the wind blew the teargas away and their attack faltered. After a fierce battle that lasted most of the afternoon, the Marines advanced slowly against heavy enemy fire. A Marine from H Company later recalled: "[The] NVA threw everything they had at us. We took incoming mortars and rockets and automatic fire." In the end, however, the Marines prevailed, killing 27 enemy soldiers and taking three prisoners, while losing one dead and 14 wounded.

A young Marine from H/2/5th Marines carries a Vietnamese woman—a patient at Hue's hospital—to safety amid the heavy fighting south of the Perfume River. (USMC/DOD)

The crew of a 106mm recoilless rifle from 2/5th Marines sets up the gun for firing to support the advance of their fellow Marines. (USMC/DOD)

The Provincial Headquarters had assumed a symbolic importance to both sides. A National Liberation Front flag had flown from the flagpole in front of the headquarters since the initial Communist takeover of the city. As a CBS television crew filmed the event, the Marines tore down the enemy ensign and raised the Stars and Stripes. This was a politically sensitive situation; the Marines should have turned over the Provincial Headquarters building to the ARVN and continued the fight, but Captain Christmas told his gunnery sergeant, "We've been looking at that damn North Vietnamese flag all day, and now we're going to take it down." A short time later, Captain Christmas received a radio call from an Army colonel in the MACV Compound ordering him to take down the American flag. He did not. Then two Army captains showed up, announcing that they were there to supervise the lowering of the flag. Christmas told them if they wanted it down so bad that they could do it themselves, but he added that he could not guarantee how his Marines, just having concluded a desperate fight to take the headquarters, would

US Marines hold a Viet Cong flag they have ripped down from atop the Thua Thien Provincial Headquarters, and replaced with the Stars and Stripes. They had recaptured the Communist stronghold after seven days of street fighting. (Bettman via Getty Images)

react. The captains took one look at the menacing Marines and quickly departed the area, leaving the flag where it was. Later, Christmas agreed to remove the flag, but only as his unit departed the area for its next objective.

To Lieutenant-Colonel Cheatham, this proved to be the turning point of the Battle of Hue south of the river. He later observed: "When we took the province headquarters, we broke their back. That was a rough one." The Provincial Headquarters had served as the command post of the 4th PAVN Regiment. With its loss, the integrity of the North Vietnamese defenses south of the river began to falter. However, the fighting was far from over.

The Nguyen Hoang Bridge (today known as Truong Tien Bridge) spanning the Perfume (Huong) River was built in 1899 to connect the new and old parts of Hue City. The bridge was blown up by Viet Cong sappers on February 7, 1968. (USMC/DOD)

On February 7, enemy sappers destroyed the Nguyen Hoang Bridge in order to prevent the Marines from using it to cross the river and attack the southeastern wall of the Citadel. However, the Navy Boat Ramp was still in operation and provided a way across the river and by February 13, Marine engineers would complete a pontoon bridge alongside the destroyed Nguyen Hoang span that would permit truck convoys to bring in much-needed supplies and food for both the troops and the civilian population.

Meanwhile, a battalion from the 327th Airborne, 101st Airborne Division was flown from III Corps to Phu Bai. There it was ordered to protect the supply point and assume the security mission in the area, thereby relieving several Marine companies for use in Hue.

By February 11, the two Marine battalions in the city had reached their objectives and were at the confluence of the Perfume River and the Phu Cam River. Two days later, Marines crossed into the western suburbs of Hue, aiming to link up with troopers of the 1st Cavalry, who were moving in toward the city. By February 14, most of the city south of the river was in American hands, but mopping-up operations would take another 12 days as rockets and mortar rounds continued to fall and isolated snipers harassed Marine patrols. Control of that sector of the city was returned to the South Vietnamese government. It had been very costly for the Marines, who sustained 38 dead and 320 wounded. It had been even more costly for the Communists; the bodies of over a thousand VC and PAVN soldiers were strewn about the city south of the river.

THE FIGHT FOR THE CITADEL

While the Marines had fought for the southern part of the city, the battle north of the Perfume River had continued to rage and the North Vietnamese were still firmly in control of most of the Citadel. Despite the efforts of the US units trying to seal off Hue from outside reinforcement, Communist troops and supplies still made it into the city from the west and north, and even on boats coming down the river. Thus, the allied forces in the city had to contend with an enemy force that was well supplied and being constantly reinforced by fresh troops. By this point in the battle, at least two additional NVA battalions had made their way into the city.

On February 2, after two days of heavy fighting, the 2nd and 7th ARVN Airborne battalions had recaptured the Tay Loc Airfield inside the Citadel, killing over 200 enemy soldiers, but in the process they also suffered heavy casualties and lost several armored personnel carriers. Nevertheless, the paratroopers pressed on toward the western wall. About 1500hrs, the 1st Battalion of the 3rd ARVN Regiment reached the Mang Ca Compound

Elements of the US 1st Air Cavalry, supported by armor, move north en route to Hue. Shortly after passing this road marker, they were ambushed by Communist forces. (Bettman via Getty Images)

and, along with Hac Bao "Black Panther" troopers, attacked toward the northwest corner. By February 4, the paratroopers had secured the An Hoa Gate in the northwest corner of the Citadel. Along the way, the Hac Bao liberated Lieutenant Tran Ngoc Hue's house; the Hac Bao commander feared for the worst when he saw that it had been destroyed by the fighting, but somehow his loved ones, battered but alive, had survived in the family bunker.

On February 3, Brigadier-General Ngo Quang Truong directed the 2nd Troop, 7th Armored Cavalry Squadron to move from Quang Tri to Hue. Upon trying to leave Quang Tri south along QL 1, the cavalry troopers in 15 armored personnel carriers ran into heavy contact and the unit became bogged down. However, by February 6, they were able to break through the enemy resistance and headed south. After stopping for the night at Camp Evans, the next morning they continued their march toward Hue. About 12km north of the city, the cavalrymen left the highway and turned east across the rice paddies, making their way to the Mang Ca Compound at 1700hrs. They were directed to take up positions around the airfield.

Meanwhile, two companies from the 4th Battalion, 2nd ARVN Regiment, which had been airlifted by US Marine CH-46 "Sea Knight" helicopters from Dong Ha, advanced south from the Mang Ca Compound toward the Imperial Palace. Marine helicopters also flew in paratroopers from the 9th Airborne Battalion from Quang Tri to join the battle. The ARVN reinforcements made some progress, but, after seven attempts to take the Ngan Gate, their attack stalled and they took up defensive positions. That night, the PAVN counterattacked and forced the ARVN troops who had attacked toward the Imperial Palace to pull back to the Tay Loc Airfield. At the same time, the North Vietnamese rushed additional reinforcements into the city. Brigadier-General Ngo Quang Truong responded by redeploying his forces, ordering the remainder of the 3rd ARVN Regiment, unable to penetrate the Citadel walls from the south, to board junks and move by water to the Mang Ca Compound.

ALLIED
1st ARVN Division
    1st Infantry Regiment
    2nd Infantry Regiment
    3rd Infantry Regiment
    7th Armored Cavalry
    Squadron
    1st Airborne Task Force
        2nd Airborne Battalion
        7th Airborne Battalion
        9th Airborne Battalion
TF X-Ray (USMC)
    1st Battalion, 1st Marine
    Regiment
    2nd Battalion, 5th Marine
    Regiment

QL 1

NGU HA
CANAL

TAY LOC
AIRFIELD

1

4

TIEU GIANG
RIVER

BACH HO
BRIDGE

EVENTS

1. February 2: The 2nd and 7th ARVN Airborne battalions recapture the Tay Loc Airfield inside the Citadel.

2. February 3: 1/1st Marines and 2/5th Marines begin to attack south and west to clear the modern city south of the Perfume River.

3. February 3: 2nd Troop, 7th Armored Cavalry Squadron arrives at Mang Ca Compound.

4. February 6: 2nd Battalion, 4th Regiment attacks toward the Imperial Palace but the advance stalls against stiff enemy resistance.

5. February 10: 1/1st Marines and 2/5th Marines reach their objectives in the western part of the modern city.

6. February 11: 1/1st Marines and 2/5th Marines reach the confluence of the Perfume and Phu Cam rivers.

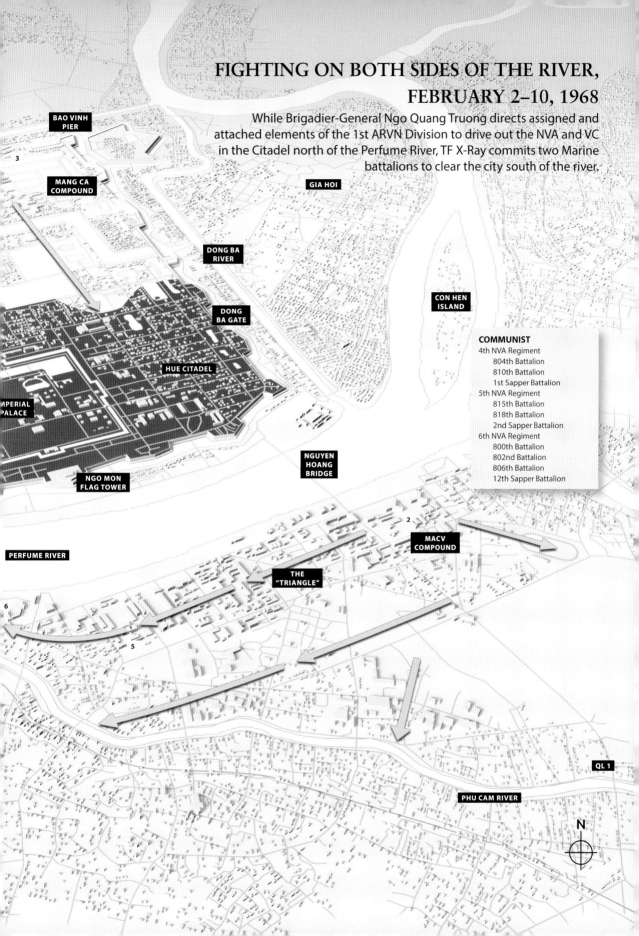

FIGHTING ON BOTH SIDES OF THE RIVER, FEBRUARY 2–10, 1968

While Brigadier-General Ngo Quang Truong directs assigned and attached elements of the 1st ARVN Division to drive out the NVA and VC in the Citadel north of the Perfume River, TF X-Ray commits two Marine battalions to clear the city south of the river.

BAO VINH PIER

3

MANG CA COMPOUND

GIA HOI

DONG BA RIVER

DONG BA GATE

CON HEN ISLAND

HUE CITADEL

IMPERIAL PALACE

COMMUNIST
4th NVA Regiment
    804th Battalion
    810th Battalion
    1st Sapper Battalion
5th NVA Regiment
    815th Battalion
    818th Battalion
    2nd Sapper Battalion
6th NVA Regiment
    800th Battalion
    802nd Battalion
    806th Battalion
    12th Sapper Battalion

NGUYEN HOANG BRIDGE

NGO MON FLAG TOWER

2

MACV COMPOUND

PERFUME RIVER

THE "TRIANGLE"

6

5

QL 1

PHU CAM RIVER

N

US Marines aboard a US Navy landing craft in transit on the Perfume River warily monitor the riverbank, ready to return fire. (USMC/DOD)

By the evening of February 7, Truong's forces inside the Citadel included four airborne battalions, the Hac Bao Company, two armored cavalry troops, the entire 3rd ARVN Regiment, the 4th Battalion from the 2nd ARVN Regiment, and a company from the 1st ARVN Regiment. However, this force had been depleted by the heavy fighting; some of the battalions had fewer than 200 effective soldiers. The 3rd Troop of the 7th Cavalry was down to just 40 men. Additionally, food and ammunition were running low. Morale was down due to exhaustion and a steady stream of casualties.

Despite the ARVN buildup inside the Citadel, Truong's troops failed to make any headway against the dug-in NVA, who had burrowed deep into the walls and tightly packed buildings. The ARVN attack north of the river had effectively stalled among the houses, alleys, and narrow streets adjacent to the Citadel wall to the northwest and southwest, leaving the Communists still in possession of the Imperial Palace and most of the surrounding area. At the same time, the NVA and VC seemed to be getting stronger as reinforcements and supplies continued to flow into the city over the southwestern wall and through the Huu Gate. With his troops stalled and the battle settling into a bloody stalemate, an embarrassed and frustrated Ngo Quang Truong was forced into appealing to III MAF for help.

On February 10, Lieutenant-General Cushman sent a message to Brigadier-General LaHue directing him to move a Marine battalion to the Citadel. Having received his orders from Cushman, LaHue ordered Major Robert H. Thompson's 1/5th Marines, to prepare for movement to Hue; he told Thompson to take his orders from Colonel Hughes, and Thompson later commented that "no one seemed to know what the actual situation was in the Citadel." He remembers that LaHue commented that it "shouldn't take more than a few days" to clear the enemy from the Citadel.

On February 11, Marine CH-46 helicopters lifted two platoons of B Company into the Tay Loc Airfield (the third platoon from the unit was forced to turn back when one of its pilots was wounded by ground fire). Thompson and the rest of the battalion traveled by convoy from Phu Bai to the MACV Compound. There Thompson met with Colonel Hughes, who gave him an update on the situation inside the Citadel and drew up a brief plan; Thompson would take companies A and C, link up with B Company at the Mang Ca Compound and then drive southward "within a zone of action that extended from the inner palace wall on the west to the Citadel wall on the east," forcing the NVA in the Citadel back toward the river.

The next day, Thompson and A Company, with five tanks attached, plus the missing platoon from B Company, boarded landing craft at the Navy Boat Ramp, crossed the Perfume River and continued along the moat to the east of the Citadel to a rundown ferry landing at the Bao Vinh Pier. They disembarked and began the march toward the ARVN compound through a breach in the northeast wall. C Company followed and soon joined the rest of the battalion at Mang Ca. D Company remained south of the river and was attached to 2/5th Marines for the time being.

On February 10, the South Vietnamese Joint General Staff (JGS) in Saigon ordered the redeployment of Ngo Quang Truong's airborne battalions. They were part of the general reserve and the JGS wanted them back in Saigon. This would leave Ngo Quang Truong critically short, so he requested that he be allocated units to take the place of the airborne. After some discussion, the JGS agreed to send two battalions of South Vietnamese Marines.

At the same time the US Marines were sending in reinforcements, two battalions of Vietnamese Marines were transported by helicopter and naval landing craft to the Bao Vinh landing; upon arrival, they were ordered to move to the eastern corner of the Citadel and prepare to sweep west, advancing along the western wall.

Once inside the Citadel, Major Thompson met with Brigadier-General Ngo Quang Truong and proposed that his Marines relieve the 1st Vietnamese Airborne Task Force in the northeastern section of the Citadel, then attack down the northeastern wall toward the Perfume River flanked on the right by 2nd Battalion, 3rd ARVN Regiment. Ngo Quang Truong agreed, but apparently was not aware that the South Vietnamese paratroopers had already pulled out of their assigned sector prematurely. When Thompson's battalion attacked the next day, it would run head-on into a strong North Vietnamese force that had reoccupied the area previously cleared by the paratroopers. In all, the North Vietnamese held the Citadel with two battalions, while a third was operating to the west, keeping the enemy supply lines open to the Citadel.

Thompson's plan called for two of his companies to attack abreast, A Company on the left next to the wall and C Company on its right; B Company would be in reserve. The attack began the next morning, February 13. A Company moved out under a bone-chilling rain, following the wall toward the distinctive archway of the Dong Ba Gate. At 0815hrs, as they neared the gate tower and with no airborne troops in sight, North Vietnamese troops opened up on the Marines with automatic weapons, B-40 rockets, and

US Marines from C/1/1st Marines engage the enemy with an M60 machine gun as they advance against the dug-in VC and NVA. (USMC/DOD)

ALLIED

1st ARVN Division
  TF Alpha, South Vietnamese Marine Corps
    1st Battalion
    4th Battalion
TF X-Ray (USMC)
  1st Battalion, 1st Marine Regiment
  1st Battalion, 5th Marine Regiment
  2nd Battalion, 5th Marine Regiment

QL 1

NGU HA CANAL

TAY LOC AIRFIELD

4

TIEU GIANG RIVER

BACH HO BRIDGE

EVENTS

1. February 11: One company from 1/5th Marines is flown into Tay Loc Airfield to join the fight to clear the Citadel.

2. February 12: 1/5th Marines headquarters and two more companies plus five attached tanks are transported by landing craft to Bao Vinh Pier and enter the Citadel.

3. February 13: 1/5th Marines launches an attack down the southeastern side of the Citadel.

4. February 14: Vietnamese Marines from TF Alpha launch attack from an area south of the 1st ARVN Division headquarters compound to the west, but the attack quickly becomes bogged down.

5. February 15: D/1/5th Marines secures Dong Ba Gate tower after intense fighting; 1/5th Marines continues the attack to clear enemy along the southern Citadel wall.

6. The Imperial Palace and the Gia Hoi area are the last remaining Communist strongholds north of the Perfume River.

7. While the intense fighting continues in the Citadel, allied forces continue to clear Communist fighters in the new city areas south of the Perfume River.

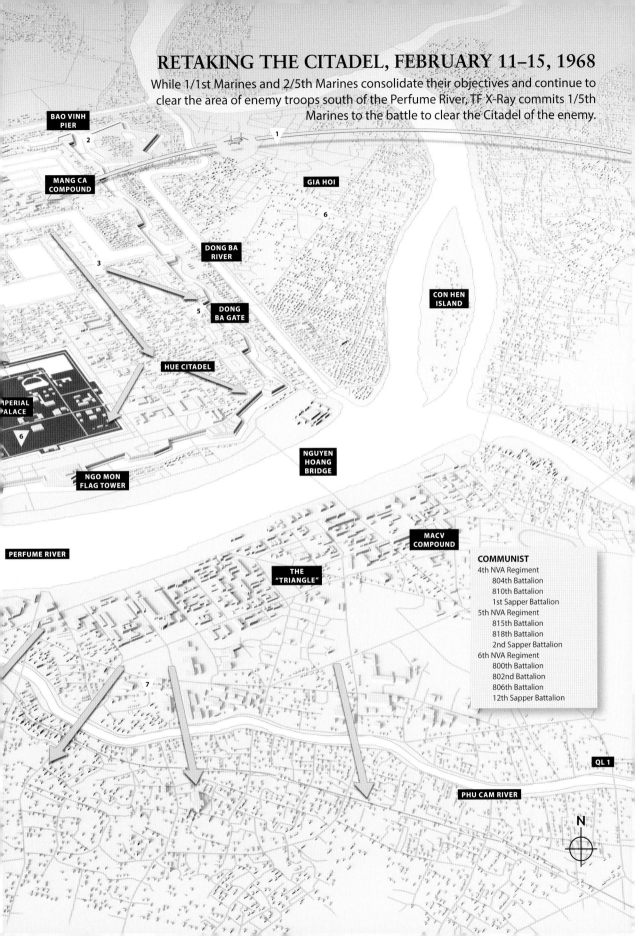

RETAKING THE CITADEL, FEBRUARY 11–15, 1968

While 1/1st Marines and 2/5th Marines consolidate their objectives and continue to clear the area of enemy troops south of the Perfume River, TF X-Ray commits 1/5th Marines to the battle to clear the Citadel of the enemy.

BAO VINH PIER

2

MANG CA COMPOUND

GIA HOI

3

DONG BA RIVER

6

DONG BA GATE

5

CON HEN ISLAND

HUE CITADEL

IMPERIAL PALACE

6

NGO MON FLAG TOWER

NGUYEN HOANG BRIDGE

PERFUME RIVER

MACV COMPOUND

THE "TRIANGLE"

7

COMMUNIST
4th NVA Regiment
    804th Battalion
    810th Battalion
    1st Sapper Battalion
5th NVA Regiment
    815th Battalion
    818th Battalion
    2nd Sapper Battalion
6th NVA Regiment
    800th Battalion
    802nd Battalion
    806th Battalion
    12th Sapper Battalion

QL 1

PHU CAM RIVER

N

mortars from houses on their right flank and from concealed positions that the enemy had dug into the base of the tower. Thompson later recalled: "all Hell broke loose. There was no Airborne unit in the area and A Company was up to their armpits in NVA."

The thick masonry of the construction of the wall and gate tower protected the enemy defenders from all the fire being brought to bear on them. Within minutes, several Marines lay dying and 30 more were wounded, including Captain John J. Bowe, Jr, the company commander. These troops, fresh from operations in Phu Loc, just north of the Hai Van Pass, were unfamiliar with both city fighting and the situation in Hue; finding themselves "surrounded by houses, gardens, stores, buildings two and three stories high, and paved roads littered with abandoned vehicles," the Marines felt out of their element.

Under heavy enemy fire, the Marine advance stalled; in the first assault on the Citadel wall, the Marines lost 15 killed and 40 wounded. Major Thompson pulled A Company back and replaced it with B Company, previously in reserve. With B Company on the left, First Lieutenant Scott A. Nelson's C Company resumed the attack with two tanks in the lead. They had gone about 300m when again they came under heavy small-arms, machine-gun, and rocket fire. The enemy had dug in at the base of the wall and the fire seemed to come from every direction.

On Thompson's right flank, the ARVN were facing the same devastating fire from snipers and entrenched enemy forces. Without heavy direct-fire weapons support, they made very little progress.

Meanwhile, after conferring with President Nguyen Van Thieu, Lieutenant-General Hoang Xuan Lam authorized allied forces to use whatever weapons were necessary to dislodge the enemy from the Citadel. Only the Imperial Palace remained off-limits for artillery and close air support.

Using the new rules of engagement, Thompson's Marines managed to inch slowly forward, using airstrikes, naval gunfire, and artillery support. Eventually, however, the attack was halted by heavy enemy fire coming from the archway tower at the Dong Ba Gate.

During the night Major Thompson requested additional artillery fire to help soften up the area for the next day's attack. He also requested that his Captain Myron "Mike" C. Harrington's D Company, still south of the river, be returned to his operational control in the Citadel.

On the morning of February 14, an array of 155mm and 8-inch howitzers and 5- and 8-inch naval guns pounded the Dong Ba Gate. At 0800hrs, following

After being given the clearance to use artillery and air support, Marines call in an air strike to support their attack on the Citadel. The ruins of one of the Citadel's gateway towers can be seen at right. (Bettman via Getty Images)

this bombardment, Thompson renewed the attack, but his Marines made little headway against the entrenched NVA and VC. That evening, Thompson ordered D Company transported to the Citadel by landing craft. The company arrived at the ramp, crossed the river under fire, and joined the rest of the battalion in the Citadel. Once Harrington and his men arrived, Thompson told him that D Company would lead the attack against the tower next morning.

US Marines attack a gateway tower in the outer wall of Hue Citadel. (Bettman via Getty Images)

On the 15th, under cover of Marine artillery, naval gunfire, and several tactical air strikes, Harrington's company, accompanied by tanks and Ontos, launched the attack against the Dong Ba Tower. After six hours of bitter close-quarter fighting, Harrington's men captured the tower, by now a pile of rubble, but only after six more Marines were killed and more than 50 wounded. That night, the PAVN retook the tower for a brief period, but Captain Harrington personally led a counterattack and took it back.

With the capture of the Dong Ba Gate tower, the American advance gained some momentum, however the Marine advance continued to be slow and deliberate. They encountered, according to Thompson, "hundreds of naturally camouflaged, mutually supporting, fortified positions." The North Vietnamese fought tenaciously, withdrawing from one house to the next in front of the deadly Marine assault. The Marines used every weapon at their disposal as they ground their way forward, but, as Thompson later observed, the enemy "had everything going for him."

South Vietnamese Marines cross the Perfume River in a landing craft to join the battle for the ancient Citadel. (Bettman via Getty Images)

As the US Marines fought their way toward the Imperial Palace, the rest of South Vietnamese Marine Task Force Alpha entered the battle. One company arrived on February 11, and the next day landing craft brought the remainder of the Vietnamese Marines from southern Hue into the Citadel. The Vietnamese Marine task force, now numbering two battalions, replaced the South Vietnamese 3rd Regiment, which moved from the southwest sector to the northwest sector of the Citadel.

At 0900hrs on the 14th, the South Vietnamese Marines launched their attack from an area south of the 1st ARVN Division headquarters compound to the west. They were then to make a left turning movement to clear the southwestern sector of the Citadel, west of the Imperial Palace. However, they did not get that far because they immediately ran into heavy resistance near the Chanh Tay Gate from strong enemy forces as they engaged in heavy house-to-house fighting. Even the addition of a third South Vietnamese Marine battalion did not help as the dug-in enemy turned back

CAPTAIN MYRON HARRINGTON'S B/1/5TH MARINES AT DONG BA GATE, FEBRUARY 15, 1968 (PP. 76–77)

On February 15, under cover of artillery, naval gunfire, and several close air support strikes, Captain Myron "Mike" Harrington's B/1/5th Marines, accompanied by tanks and Ontos, launched its attack against the Dong Ba Gate tower in the northeastern Citadel wall. After six hours of bitter close-quarter fighting, Harrington's men captured the gate tower (1), by now a pile of rubble, but only after six more Marines were killed and more than 50 wounded. That night, the PAVN retook the tower for a brief period, but Captain Harrington personally led a counterattack that took it back.

Shown here are Harrington's Marines as they advance against the dug-in Communist positions in the ruins of the gate tower. US artillery and mortar strikes (2) are hitting the area around the tower. To the right, a Marine M60 machine gunner (3) is providing covering fire. One of the advancing Marine riflemen has just thrown an M26A1 hand grenade (4). In the lower left, an injured Marine is being tended to by a comrade (5).

Following helicopter insertion, elements of Task Force Alpha of the South Vietnamese Marine Corps head for cover prior to entering Hue Citadel. (USMC/DOD)

every attack. During the next two days, the South Vietnamese advanced less than 400m. The lack of heavy direct fire weapons, especially 106mm recoilless rifles, limited the South Vietnamese ability to advance in the face of the well-entrenched enemy, and well-positioned enemy pockets were able to halt the progress of their attack.

To the north of the Vietnamese Marines, the 3rd ARVN Infantry Regiment in the northwest sector of the Citadel was also making little progress. On February 14, the enemy forces broke out of their salient west of the Tay Loc Airfield and cut off the 1st Battalion, 3rd ARVN Regiment in the western corner of the Citadel. It would take two days for the ARVN to break the encirclement, and then only after bitter fighting.

On February 15, General Creighton Abrams assumed command of MACV Forward Headquarters, which had become operational at Phu Bai three days earlier. The new command would exercise tactical authority over all American combat units north of the Hai Van Pass, giving General Westmoreland more control over the fighting in northern I CTZ. There had long been tension between Westmoreland and the Marines in I CTZ and the establishment of this new headquarters senior to III MAF would not lessen that situation.

For those still fighting in Hue, the tension between the senior commands was of little importance. On February 16, Thompson's 1/5th Marines continued its push southeast along the Citadel wall. The bloody hand-to-hand fighting went on relentlessly; the Marines inched forward, but at a great cost—seven Marines were killed and 47 wounded during that day's fighting while the enemy sustained 47 dead.

For the next seven days, the battle seesawed back and forth while much of the Citadel was pounded by close air support, artillery, and naval gunfire. The Marines were operating in a defender's paradise—row after row of densely packed, single-story, thick-walled masonry houses jammed against a solid wall riddled with spider holes and other enemy fighting positions. Each house

US Marines follow an M48 Patton tank as it advances up a residential street near the outer wall of the Citadel. (Bettman via Getty Images)

A corpsman treats the head wound of a North Vietnamese soldier found during the fight for the outer wall of the Citadel. (Bettman via Getty Images)

had its own foxholes and bunkers constructed by the residents for their own protection. Thus, each structure became a separate defensive position and each block a "formidable bastion."

The North Vietnamese fought doggedly, making the Marines pay dearly for every inch of ground gained. Even the death of the senior North Vietnamese commander in the Citadel by an artillery strike on February 16 did not shake the enemy's resolve. That night, the new North Vietnamese commander radioed his higher headquarters, requesting permission to abandon the city. He cited the high casualty rate, but his superiors told him to stand and fight. So the bitter fighting continued.

The Marines were just as determined as the North Vietnamese soldiers; they pressed forward against the entrenched enemy. The result was a bloody battle fought inch by inch, foot by foot; each enemy strongpoint had to be reduced one by one. No sooner had one position been taken than the North Vietnamese opened up from another.

M48A3 tanks and M50 Ontos were available, but these tracked vehicles found it extremely difficult to maneuver in the narrow streets and tight alleys of the Citadel. At first, the 90mm tank guns were ineffective against the concrete and stone houses; the shells often ricocheted off the thick walls back toward the Marines. The Marine tankers then switched to concrete-piercing fused shells that "resulted in excellent penetration and walls were breached with two to four rounds." Then the tanks proved invaluable in assisting the infantry assault. One Marine rifleman later stated, "If it had not been for the tanks, we could not have pushed through that section of the city. [The North Vietnamese] seemed to have bunkers everywhere."

As a result of the intense fighting, Hue was being reduced to rubble, block by block. Many of the enemy dead and wounded were trapped in the ruined homes and shattered courtyards. Enemy troops killed by the Marines and South Vietnamese troops lay where they had fallen. One of the MACV advisors later wrote: "The bodies, bloated and vermin infested, attracted rats and stray dogs. So, because of public health concerns, details were formed to bury the bodies as quickly as possible." For those who fought in Hue, the stench and horrors of the corpses and the rats would never be forgotten.

As the brutal battle for the Citadel raged, General Abrams met on February 16 with generals Cushman, LaHue, and Hoang Xuan Lam at MACV Forward Headquarters at Phu Bai to discuss the situation. Also in attendance were South Vietnamese Vice President Nguyen Cao Ky, who had arrived to receive a report on the battle for Hue. The MACV Forward staff and Brigadier-General LaHue briefed the dignitaries on the battle for the city; they told Abrams and the assembled group that intelligence indicated that the enemy might be preparing to move units from Khe Sanh to join the fight in Hue. Nguyen Cao Ky agreed with this assessment, saying that the North Vietnamese were willing to sacrifice "thousands of men to win a slight political gain." He then declared that US forces should not let enemy use of

An exhausted corpsman atop a Marine M50 Ontos takes a much-needed break during the intense fighting. (USMC/DOD)

pagodas, churches, or other religious buildings deter their advance and that he would "accept responsibility" for any destruction, if it was necessary to drive the enemy out of the Citadel.

Meanwhile, the fighting in the city continued unabated; 1/5th Marines had suffered 47 killed and 240 wounded in just seven days of fighting. Even the chaplain, Father Aloysius McGonigal, was killed. One Marine wrote after the battle: "On the worst days, no one expected to get through it alive." Constantly under fire for the whole time, the Marines, numb with fatigue, kept up the fight despite having slept only in three-to four-hour snatches during the battle and most not even stopping to eat. Major Thompson would remark after the battle: "The Marines were magnificent, not so much for their skills, but their raw courage in overcoming unbelievable obstacles in accomplishing their mission."

The fighting was so intense that the corpsmen and doctors had a very difficult time keeping up with the casualties. To take the place of the mounting casualties, Marine replacements were brought in during the battle, but many of them were killed or wounded before their squad leaders could even learn their names. Some replacements arrived in Hue directly upon their completion of infantry training at Camp Pendleton, California. The rapid rate of attrition was evident in that there were Marine KIAs found still wearing their stateside fatigues and boots.

It was later learned that the enemy were having their own problems. On the

Marines stay low to avoid Communist fire as they bring forward a stretcher for a wounded corpsman in Hue Citadel. (Bettman via Getty Images)

night of February 14, a US Marine forward observer with ARVN troops inside the Citadel, monitoring enemy radio frequencies, learned that the PAVN were planning a battalion-size attack by reinforcements through the west gate of the Citadel. The forward observer called in Marine 155mm howitzers and all available naval gunfire on pre-planned targets around one of the western gates and the moat bridge leading to it. The forward observer reported that he had heard "screaming on the radio" as he monitored the PAVN net. Later, it was confirmed by additional radio intercepts that the artillery and naval gunfire had caught the North Vietnamese battalion coming across the moat bridge, killing a high-ranking North Vietnamese officer and a large number of the fresh troops.

On February 17, with what was left of his battalion completely exhausted and nearly out of food and ammunition, Major Thompson chose to rest his troops in preparation for a renewal of the attack. They needed time to clean their weapons, stock up on ammunition, tend the walking wounded, and gird themselves for the next round of bitter fighting.

The Marines resumed their attack on February 18, but continued to meet heavy resistance from the enemy, who were still receiving replacements and supplies from the outside. Still, the Marines pressed the attack, inching forward against the entrenched enemy.

On February 20, General Abrams, saying that he believed the effort by the Marines in the Citadel to be "inadequate," wanted to relieve Thompson. When Colonel Hughes learned of this, he told Abrams that he would resign before he would relieve Thompson. Nothing more was said about the relief and Thompson stayed in command of his Marines.

It had been a tough fight and Thompson realized that his force was worn out; he and his Marines had advanced only four blocks and were still two blocks from the southeastern wall of the Citadel. He decided he would try something new. To the battalion's front there was a large, two-story building, surrounded by a large courtyard. The building, the largest in the Citadel, and two smaller adjacent structures provided the North Vietnamese clear fields of fire on the Marine advance. Accordingly, Thompson came up with a plan to send out a night raid to seize the building complex to cover the battalion's attack in daylight the next morning.

In the early morning hours of February 21, three small groups of Marines from A Company, now commanded by First Lieutenant Patrick D. Polk, crept toward the three buildings that had been key to the enemy's defenses. To their surprise, they found the buildings virtually undefended. It appeared that the enemy had withdrawn from these forward positions during the night to get some rest. Just before first light the next morning, the enemy returned to reoccupy their positions only to find Thompson's Marines waiting on them. As the Marines from A Company opened fire on the PAVN, Lieutenant Polk and his forward observer called in mortars on the North Vietnamese. After more than an hour of being pounded by high-explosive rounds and CS gas, 19 PAVN soldiers lay dead. The rest of Thompson's battalion moved forward toward the Huu Gate, the last remaining entrance to the Citadel in NVA hands. Despite their surprise, the enemy recovered quickly and put up a stiff defense. By the end of the day, the Marines prevailed, but they were still about a hundred meters short of the southeastern wall; that day's fighting resulted in three Marines killed and 14 wounded.

As the fighting raged inside the Citadel, US intelligence determined that the PAVN and VC were staging out of a base camp 18km west of the city and that reinforcements from that area were entering the fortress using the Huu Gate. Additionally, a new enemy battalion had been identified west of the city and a new regimental headquarters was thought to be 2km north of the city with at least one battalion.

Acting on this intelligence, General Abrams and Lieutenant-General Cushman decided that Hue had to be sealed from outside reinforcements if the Marines and ARVN were to root out the enemy in the Citadel. Accordingly, they placed the 1st Brigade, 101st Airborne Division with two battalions under the operational control of TF X-Ray. The paratroopers would be tasked with defending Phu Bai while the Marines focused on the battle for Hue. At the same time, the 3rd Brigade of the 1st Cavalry Division would be reinforced with two more battalions and was ordered to launch coordinated assaults on the city from their blocking positions to the northwest.

A Marine from 1/5th Marines cleans his M16 rifle during a lull in the fighting. The M16 made its debut in the Vietnam War, and its reliability during the early stages of the conflict was questionable, made worse by a lack of cleaning kits. Although marketed as a "self-cleaning" rifle, routine cleaning and lubrication were essential to prevent malfunction. (USMC/DOD)

For almost three weeks, 1st Cavalry endeavored to cut off the reinforcement of Hue by North Vietnamese troops from the PAVN 24th, 29th, and 99th regiments. On February 19, the 2nd Battalion, 501st Infantry (2/501st Infantry), attached to the 3rd Brigade, was ordered to move south from Camp Evans to PK-17. Also on that day, the 1/7th Cavalry, relieved from its base defense mission at Camp Evans, deployed south to the Hue area. The 3rd Brigade then had four battalions at its disposal and prepared to attack eastward toward Hue; 1/7th Cavalry and 5/7th Cavalry were to attack toward Thon Que Chu, 2/501st Infantry was to advance in the center while 2/12th Cavalry would advance northward.

On February 21, the 1st Cavalry troopers attacked. The contact with the enemy became increasingly heavy as they got closer to Hue. With naval gunfire, artillery, and helicopter gunships, the troopers slowly pushed the enemy back. By dark, the 1st Cavalry troops were within 5km of the city.

The next morning, three battalions continued the attack eastward while 1/7th Cavalry remained in the area to clean out bypassed enemy pockets of resistance. For the next two days, the troopers pressed the attack, overcoming very heavy resistance in the move to seal off the western wall of the Citadel. This finally deprived the North Vietnamese of incoming supplies and reinforcements and precipitated a rapid deterioration of the enemy's strength inside the Citadel. The North Vietnamese were now fighting a rearguard action, but they still fought for every inch of ground and continued to throw replacements into the fight.

THE FINAL PUSH

As elements of the 1st Cavalry advanced toward Hue from the west and action continued inside the Citadel, fire support coordination became a major concern. On February 21, Brigadier-General Oscar E. Davis, one of the

The fight for Hue Citadel, February 2–25, 1968

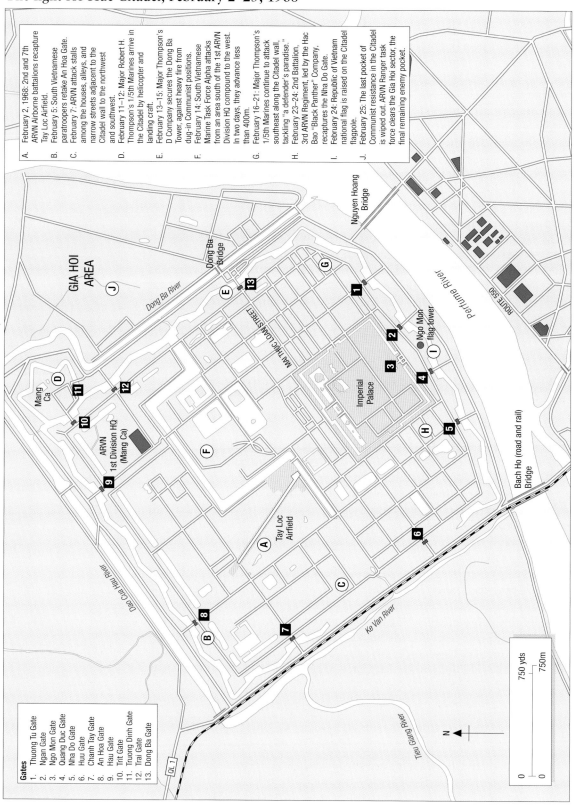

A. February 2, 1968: 2nd and 7th ARVN Airborne battalions recapture Tay Loc Airfield.
B. February 5: South Vietnamese paratroopers retake An Hoa Gate.
C. February 7: ARVN attack stalls among the houses, alleys, and narrow streets adjacent to the Citadel wall to the northwest and southwest.
D. February 11–12: Major Robert H. Thompson's 1/5th Marines arrive in the Citadel by helicopter and landing craft.
E. February 13–15: Major Thompson's D Company secures the Dong Ba Tower, against heavy fire from dug-in Communist positions.
F. February 14: South Vietnamese Marine Task Force Alpha attacks from an area south of the 1st ARVN Division HQ compound to the west. In two days, they advance less than 400m.
G. February 16–21: Major Thompson's 1/5th Marines continue to attack southeast along the Citadel wall, tackling "a defender's paradise."
H. February 23–24: 2nd Battalion, 3rd ARVN Regiment, led by the Hac Bao "Black Panther" Company, recaptures the Nha Do Gate.
I. February 24: Republic of Vietnam national flag is raised on the Citadel flagpole.
J. February 25: The last pocket of Communist resistance in the Citadel is wiped out. ARVN Ranger task force clears the Gia Hoi sector, the final remaining enemy pocket.

Gates
1. Thuong Tu Gate
2. Ngan Gate
3. Ngo Mon Gate
4. Quang Duc Gate
5. Nha Do Gate
6. Huu Gate
7. Chanh Tay Gate
8. An Hoa Gate
9. Hau Gate
10. Trit Gate
11. Truong Dinh Gate
12. Trai Gate
13. Dong Ba Gate

84

two assistant division commanders for the 1st Cavalry, flew into the Citadel to assess the situation. Co-locating his headquarters with Brigadier-General Ngo Quang Truong in the 1st ARVN Division headquarters compound in Mang Ca, Davis assumed the role of the overall area fire support coordinator.

For the final assault on the Imperial Palace itself, Thompson's battalion received a fresh unit, Captain John D. Niotis's L/1/5th Marines. By February 22, the Communists held only the southwestern corner of the Citadel. At 0930hrs that morning, the 1st Battalion launched the final assault on the southeastern wall with A Company in the lead. It quickly became apparent that the enemy had melted away. Against only sporadic mortar and sniper fire, the Marines secured the wall. Lance Corporal James Avella took a small American flag from his pack and fastened it to "a sagging telegraph pole."

With the southeastern wall secured, Thompson directed Captain Niotis and Company L to continue the attack to capture the Ngo Mon Gate and the immediate area outside the Citadel leading to the Bach Ho Bridge across the Perfume River. With Marine aircraft dropping napalm within 800m in front of them and supported by tank fire, L Company launched the attack. It pushed through a row of houses, the Marines throwing grenades in the windows before rushing the houses. Steadily advancing against "enemy contact [that] was lighter than any previous offensive day," the Marines captured all their assigned objectives by 1800hrs.

Major Thompson hoped to take part in the final assault to take the Imperial Palace, but it was decided that it was more politically expedient to have the Palace liberated by South Vietnamese forces, rather than US Marines. He later observed: "I was not allowed to do it. To save face, the Vietnamese were to retake the 'Forbidden City'."

However, the South Vietnamese forces were having a difficult time. To the west of the American Marines, the South Vietnamese Marines were still dealing with the enemy, who continued to fight for almost every part of the old city still in their hands. At one point, the NVA launched a counterattack; although the South Vietnamese Marines, supported by 8-inch and 105mm artillery fire, drove the enemy back after a two-hour battle, they were not able to advance, gaining less than half a city block in three days of heavy fighting.

On the night of February 23/24, to relieve pressure on the South Vietnamese Marines, the 2nd Battalion, 3rd ARVN Regiment, led by the "Hac Bao" Black Panther Company, launched a surprise attack westward along the wall in the southeastern section of the Citadel. The North Vietnamese were caught off guard, but quickly recovered. A savage battle ensued, but the South Vietnamese pressed the attack, eventually recapturing the Nha Do Gate. The Communists, deprived of their supply centers to the west by the link-up between the 1st Cavalry and 2/5th Marines, fell back.

Marines of A/3/5th Marines make effective use of walls and buildings for cover as they advance against the Communist positions in Hue. (USMC/DOD)

South Vietnamese soldiers raise the Republic of Vietnam national flag over the Citadel after 25 days of bitter fighting. (USMC/DOD)

South Vietnamese President Nguyen Van Thieu (left) hands out towels to an elderly refugee during his visit to battle-scarred Hue. (Bettman via Getty Images)

Included in the ground gained by the South Vietnamese attack was the Ngo Mon flag tower. At 0500hrs on the 24th, South Vietnamese troops from the Hac Bao Company and the 2nd Battalion, 3rd Regiment ripped down the large NLF flag that had flown over the Citadel for 25 days. The ARVN soldiers gleefully hoisted the yellow and triple red-striped Republic of Vietnam national flag in its place.

By 1025hrs that morning, elements of the 3rd ARVN Regiment had reached the southern wall and secured it. General Truong then ordered the Hac Bao Company and the 2nd Battalion of the 3rd Regiment to continue the attack to secure the Imperial Palace. Supported by US Marine tanks, M50 Ontos, and recoilless rifles, the South Vietnamese launched their attack, with the Black Panthers in the vanguard. Lieutenant Tran Ngoc Hue, and his advisor Captain James Cooligan, led the Hac Bao on a frontal assault across open ground. The Marines, who were normally not very impressed by the combat prowess of the South Vietnamese, were stunned at the sheer audacity of the attack; watching the assault, one Marine exclaimed: "Man, have those guys got balls!" By late afternoon, the South Vietnamese troops had secured the palace and its surrounding grounds.

At this point, the NVA held only the southwest corner of the Citadel. At 0300hrs on February 25, the 4th Vietnamese Marine Battalion launched a surprise attack and quickly eliminated the final pocket of enemy resistance in the Citadel, but not without losing 15 killed in the process. With the loss of their last toehold in the Citadel, the surviving VC and North Vietnamese troops fled westward; they had sustained 178 killed in action during the South Vietnamese Marine attack. On the other side of the Citadel, beyond its northeastern walls, an ARVN Ranger task force under Captain Pham Van Phuoc, cleared the Gia Hoi area, the last remaining enemy pocket. Fighting in the areas surrounding the city continued for another week, but the battle for Hue City proper was largely over.

On February 26, South Vietnamese President Nguyen Van Thieu, himself a former commander of the 1st ARVN Division, flew into Hue to congratulate Brigadier-General Ngo Quang Truong and his troops on their victory. On March 2, 1968, Operation *Hue City* was officially terminated. It had been a bitter and bloody ordeal that lasted for 25 days.

US/ARVN unit dispositions, February 24–25, 1968

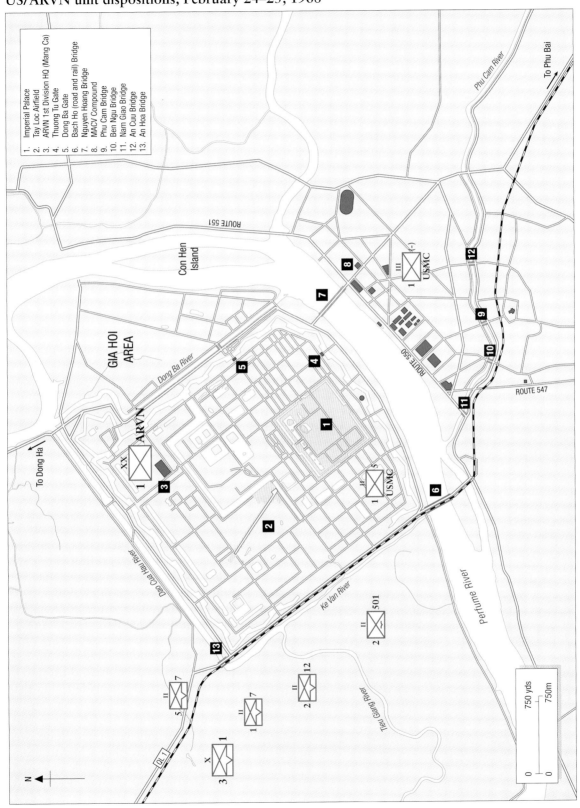

1. Imperial Palace
2. Tay Loc Airfield
3. ARVN 1st Division HQ (Mang Ca)
4. Thuong Tu Gate
5. Dong Ba Gate
6. Bach Ho (road and rail) Bridge
7. Nguyen Hoang Bridge
8. MACV Compound
9. Phu Cam Bridge
10. Ben Ngu Bridge
11. Nam Giao Bridge
12. An Cuu Bridge
13. An Hoa Bridge

AFTERMATH

The Battle of Hue was the longest sustained infantry battle of the war to that point. As with many battles in the Vietnam War, both sides claimed victory. The Communists had taken and held the city for three weeks, claiming an "unprecedented victory of scientific quality." From the allied perspective, the fighting had been intense and bloody, but in the end the allies had ejected the Communists and recaptured the city.

Allied estimates of NVA and VC dead ranged from 2,500 to 5,000 troops killed in the city, while another 3,000 reportedly fell in the fighting in the areas surrounding the city. Captured Communist documents admitted to 1,042 killed and an undisclosed number of wounded. Regardless of the exact figures, the enemy had suffered horribly in the brutal fighting. A captured document later revealed that the Communists had lost one regimental, eight battalion and 24 company commanders, as well as 72 platoon leaders in the bitter fighting.

The cost had also been very high for the allies. In the 26 days of combat in Hue, the ARVN lost 333 killed and more than 1,700 wounded, plus 30 missing in action; the Vietnamese Marines lost 88 killed and 350 wounded. The US Marines suffered 142 dead and another 1,100 were wounded, while the US Army sustained 74 dead and 509 wounded in the battles that raged in and around the city.

Although the US command had tried to limit damage to the city by relying on extremely accurate 8-inch howitzers and naval gunfire, the house-to-house fighting took its toll and much of the once-beautiful city lay in rubble. In the 25 days of fighting to retake Hue, 40 percent of the city was destroyed, and 116,000 civilians were made homeless (out of a pre-Tet population of 140,000).

In urban warfare, the people are often caught in the middle between the two opposing forces. Hue was no exception. The initial attack provided the first trickle of civilians seeking refuge in the relative safety of the MACV Compound. The trickle would become a flood over the next weeks, creating a logistical and security nightmare for the US and South Vietnamese forces in Hue. Every turn in the fighting flushed out hundreds

After the bitter battle for Hue, a South Vietnamese soldier gazes up at a one-story-tall cardboard figure of a gunfighter used to advertise a movie theater in the city. The violence on the screen paled in comparison to the battle that had raged in the city for 25 days. (Bettman via Getty Images)

of Vietnamese civilians of every age. Whole families were able to survive the shelling and street warfare by taking refuge in small bunkers they had constructed in their homes. Out of the rubble came old men, women, and children, waving pieces of white cloth attached to sticks. The refugee problem reached staggering proportions; something had to be done about this growing flood of refugees and displaced persons as the battle continued to rage.

Army Major Jack E. Walker, from the Thua Thien Sector advisory team, was placed in charge of coordinating the effort to manage the refugee situation. Temporary housing was found at a complex near the MACV Compound and at Hue University, where the number of refugees swelled to 22,000. Another 40,000 displaced persons were in the Citadel area across the river. Most of the refugees were innocent civilians, but many were ARVN troops trapped at home on leave for the Tet holidays. All of these ARVN soldiers who were fit for duty were put to use helping the Marines and MACV advisors with the refugees.

In addition to dealing with shelter for the refugees, US and South Vietnamese officials had to restore city services, including water and power; provide food; and eliminate health hazards, including burying the dead. With the assistance of the local Catholic hierarchy and American resources and personnel, the South Vietnamese government officials tried to restore order and normalcy in the city. By the end of February, a full-time refugee administrator was in place and the local government slowly began to function once more.

More than the loss of their homes and businesses, the civilian population also suffered terrible loss of life, with 5,800 reported killed or missing during the 25 days of bitter fighting. Approximately 1,200 of these fatalities died from errant bombs or in the deadly house-to-house fighting. However, there were several thousand civilians that were unaccounted for when the battle was over. Shortly after the battle ended, several graves were found on the campuses of the Gia Long and Gia Hoi high schools and in the vicinity of the Tang Quang Tu Pagoda. During the weeks and months that followed the battle, South Vietnamese authorities and American

ABOVE LEFT
Looking down from a gate tower in Hue Citadel, this is the war-torn scene in the once-beautiful ancient city. About 70 percent of the houses were destroyed during the battle for control of South Vietnam's second most important city. An M48 Patton tank can be seen in the lower left. (Bettman via Getty Images)

ABOVE RIGHT
Refugees whose homes have been wrecked during the bloody 25-day battle for the Imperial City start to erect a crude shelter as they contemplate rebulding their homes and lives. (Bettman via Getty Images)

A grief-stricken mother weeps beside the coffins of her two sons who were executed by Communist forces during the fighting in Hue. (© Hulton-Deutsch Collection/CORBIS/Corbis via Getty Images)

Bereaved relatives mourn their dead beside rows of coffins of victims of the 1968 Tet Offensive. This mass funeral of 250 people killed by Communist forces was held in October 1969, the bodies having been only recently discovered that year. (Bettman via Getty Images)

soldiers discovered a series of mass graves in and around the city of Hue, some pinpointed by enemy prisoners, while others were discovered by US troops during the course of subsequent combat operations.

Nearly 3,000 corpses were found in these graves—most shot, bludgeoned to death, or buried alive, almost all with their hands tied behind their backs. Those killed included soldiers, civil servants, merchants, clergymen, schoolteachers, intellectuals, and foreigners; most of these victims were among those that Viet Cong cadre had rounded up as "cruel tyrants and puppet administrators" soon after taking the city. The full story of what happened in Hue may never be known, but it was presumed that those found in the mass graves were systematically executed by the VC and NVA during the battle or as they withdrew from the Citadel.

The Battle of Hue was a bloody affair that resulted in a severe casualty toll. It was only through the valor of the individual Marines and soldiers, both American and South Vietnamese, that the allies prevailed against a determined enemy under combat conditions in an urban environment that far exceeded anything that any of them had previously experienced. However, the victory at Hue did not prove decisive in the long run. Despite the overwhelming tactical victory achieved by the allies in the city and on the other battlefields throughout South Vietnam, the Tet Offensive proved to be a strategic defeat for the United States.

US public opinion, no doubt influenced in large part by the media coverage, especially that of the bloody fighting in Hue, began to shift away from support for the war. CBS television news anchor Walter Cronkite, who had witnessed first-hand the fighting in Hue, no doubt voiced the sentiment of many Americans when he exclaimed: "What the hell is going on? I thought we were winning the war." On February 27, after returning from Vietnam, Cronkite went on the air, declared the war a stalemate, and called for the US to negotiate its way out of the war.

CBS News correspondent Walter Cronkite reporting from Hue during the 1968 Tet Offensive. After returning to the United States, he would tell his audience that he thought the war had reached a stalemate. (CBS via Getty Images)

On March 31, 1968, the full impact of the Tet Offensive was demonstrated when President Lyndon Baines Johnson announced a halt to all bombing of North Vietnam above the 20th Parallel. Then, in a surprise move, the President declared that he would not seek re-election to a second term in the White House. Thus, the Communists, having been soundly defeated on the battlefield, nonetheless won a great strategic victory. The Tet Offensive resulted in a sea change in US policy in Vietnam and the United States soon began its long bloody disengagement from the war that would see the final departure of all American troops in early 1973 and the fall of Saigon two years later.

THE BATTLEFIELD TODAY

Today, Hue is a popular tourist center. It is the intellectual, cultural, and spiritual heart of Vietnam. In addition to being the site of the cataclysmic battle in 1968, it is more famous in recent times for its historic monuments, which have earned it a UNESCO World Heritage Site designation. Among these sites are the Citadel, the opulent tombs of the Nguyen Dynasty and the Tien Mu Pagoda, one of the most iconic structures in Vietnam. Although a lot of the city on both sides of the Perfume River was severely damaged in the three-week long battle in 1968, most areas have been largely restored.

Visitors can access the 4km-square Citadel, with its fortified gates and surrounding moat, from the southern part of the city via the Phu Xuan Bridge over the Perfume River, entering the Citadel through the Ngan Gate (Cua Ngan). Once through the gate, a short walk along 23 Thang 8 Street takes you to the Ngo Mon Gate, which serves as the entrance to the Imperial Palace. Across from that entrance is the 37m-high Ngo Mon flag tower, from which the National Liberation Front flag was raised after the North Vietnamese occupied the city. Today, the red, single star national flag of the Socialist Republic of Vietnam flies from it.

The Imperial Palace was once a complex of palaces and pavilions where civil and religious ceremonies took place. Inside the palace was the

In this picture taken on January 18, 2018, tourists visit the Purple Forbidden City within the Imperial Palace in Hue Citadel. (HOANG DINH NAM/ AFP via Getty Images)

In this picture taken in 2018, motorcyclists ride past the Ngo Mon flag tower on the southeastern walls of Hue Citadel. The flag tower faces opposite the principal entrance to the walled Imperial Palace, the Ngo Mon Gate. (HOANG DINH NAM/AFP via Getty Images)

Forbidden Purple City, to which only the emperors, concubines, and those close enough to them were granted access; the punishment for trespassing was death.

In 1968, this area was the site of several weeks of intense fighting as the Marines and South Vietnamese forces fought to oust the North Vietnamese and VC troops. Although many priceless monuments and relics were destroyed in the fighting, many survived and have been preserved for viewing. Today, little of the original Forbidden Purple City remains, though reconstruction efforts are in progress to restore and maintain it as a historic tourist attraction.

In the northern corner of the Citadel stands the Mang Ca Compound, which was the headquarters of the 1st ARVN Division during the 1968 Tet Offensive. Today, it is still used by the Vietnamese military and is not open to the public.

Exiting the Imperial Palace to the northeast through the ornate Hien Nhan Mon Gate and taking a right on Doan Thi Diem Street to Le Truc Street, visitors will find the Museum of Royal Fine Arts, which includes a collection of miscellaneous royal artifacts and other objects.

Across the street from the Royal Fine Arts museum can be found the Hue Provincial Museum. The central building includes archaeological discoveries from Thua Thien Province. To the left of the central building is a pavilion dedicated to the history of the First Indochina War. The building on the right is dedicated to the Second Indochina War, which includes a large topographical map depicting the movements of both sides during the 1968 Tet Offensive. Outside in the open, there are a number of pieces of abandoned military equipment.

The Ho Chi Minh Museum is located at 9 D Le Loi Street. The museum contains photographs, some of Ho Chi Minh's personal effects, and documents relating to his life. Another site of note is the National School (Quoc Hoc) at 10 D Le Loi Street. Founded in 1896, it was run by Ngo Dinh Kha, the father of South Vietnamese president Ngo Dinh Diem. The school was attended by several men who rose to prominence in both North and South Vietnam, to include General Vo Nguyen Giap and North Vietnam's premier during the war and after, Pham Van Dong. The school was also briefly attended by Ho Chi Minh in 1908.

Along the Perfume River, on both banks, there are several other monuments, including the tombs of seven emperors from the Nguyen Dynasty, including Minh Mang, Khai Dinh, Tu Duc, and, most importantly, Gia Long, the founder of the dynasty. Roughly 3km southwest of the Citadel, on the northern riverbank, is the Tien Mu Pagoda, which includes a seven-story octagonal tower. Tien Mu is the largest Buddhist pagoda in Hue and the official symbol of the city. It was also the home of Thich Quang Dich, the Mahayna Buddhist monk who immolated himself on June 11, 1963 in protest against the Ngo Dinh Diem regime; there is an altar honoring the

The Imperial Palace looking north through the Ngo Mon Gate, within Hue Citadel. (Chrix LOVINY/Gamma-Rapho via Getty Images)

martyred monk in the grounds of the pagoda. The best way to visit the pagoda and other sites along the river is by cruise boat.

In addition to the various touristic attractions in Hue itself, local travel companies also offer day trips to the former Demilitarized Zone lying approximately 70km north. Also within a day's journey are various other war sites, including Quang Tri (the site of heavy fighting in both 1968 and the spring of 1972), Con Thien, Camp Carroll, the Rockpile, and Khe Sanh Combat Base (45km northwest of Hue on Route AH16). With the exception of Khe Sanh, where there is a small museum and various weapons displays, visitors should not expect to see much evidence remaining from the war. For example, the site of Camp Carroll is now a pepper plantation.

While in Hue, tours can also be arranged to the Vinh Moc tunnels, located 20km north of what was the DMZ. There, the villagers built a 3km-long network of tunnels to escape American bombing. Today, there are guided tours of the tunnel complex and there is a small museum on site.

The ornate Hien Nhan Mon Gate on the northeastern side of the Imperial Palace walls within Hue Citadel. The gateway still stands today. (USMC/DOD)

South of Hue between the city and Da Nang lies the famous Hai Van Pass, which lies on National Route 1A along Vietnam's coastline. The road, twisting and turning as it ascends and then descends the pass, is quite dangerous, but the views, especially from the pass, are spectacular. The pass figured prominently during the Vietnam War since it was astride the major line of communication from Da Nang to the DMZ, called by the French "The Street without Joy." There are the remains of an old French bunker from the First Indochina War at the top of the pass.

BIBLIOGRAPHY

Arnold, James R., *Tet Offensive 1968: Turning Point in Vietnam* (London, 1990)

Bowden, Mark, *Hue 1968: A Turning Point of the American War in Vietnam* (New York, 2017)

Braestrup, Peter, *Big Story* (Boulder, CO, 1977)

Ca, Nha and Dor, Olga, *Mourning Headband for Hue: An Account of the Battle of Hue, Vietnam 1968* (Bloomington, IN, 2014)

Conboy, Ken, Bowra, Ken, and McCouaig, Simon, *The NVA and Viet Cong* (London, 1991)

Cosmas, Graham A., *MACV: The Joint Command in the Years of Withdrawal, 1968–1973* (Washington DC, 2007)

Ford, Ronnie E., *Tet 1968: Understanding the Surprise* (London, 1995)

Hammel, Eric M., *Fire in the Streets: The Battle of Hue, Tet 1968* (Chicago, 1991)

——, *Marines in Hue City: A Portrait of Urban Combat, Tet 1968* (St Paul, MN, 2007)

Krohn, Charles A., *The Lost Battalion: Controversy and Casualties in the Battle of Hue* (Westport, CN, 1993)

Laurence, John, *The Cat From Hue: A Vietnam War Story* (New York, 2002)

Luong, Colonel H., *The General Offensives of 1968–69* (Washington DC, 1981)

Moïse, Edwin E., *The Myths of Tet: The Most Misunderstood Event of the Vietnam War* (Lawrence, KS, 2017)

Murphy, Edward F., *Semper Fi: From Da Nang to the DMZ, Marine Corps Campaigns, 1965–1975* (Novato, CA, 1997)

Nguyen, Lien-Hang T., *Hanoi's War: An International History of the War for Peace in Vietnam* (Chapel Hill, NC, 2012)

Nolan, Keith William, *Battle for Hue: Tet, 1968* (Novato, CA, 1983)

Oberdorfer, Don, *Tet!* (New York, 1971)

Pearson, Willard, *The War in the Northern Provinces, 1966–1968* (Washington DC, 1975)

Rottman, Gordon L., *Viet Cong Fighter* (Oxford, UK, 2007)

——, *North Vietnamese Army Soldier 1958–75* (Oxford, UK, 2009)

——, *Army of the Republic of Vietnam 1955–75* (Oxford, UK, 2010)

Schmitz, David F., *The Tet Offensive: Politics, War, and Public Opinion* (Lanham, MD, 2005)

Shulimson, Jack, Blasiol, Leonard A., Smith, Charles R., and Dawson, David A., *US Marines in Vietnam: The Defining Year 1968* (Washington DC, 1997)

Smith, George W., *The Siege at Hue* (New York, 2000)

Son, Pham Van, *Tet – 1968* (Salisbury, NC, 1980)

Stanton, Shelby, *Anatomy of a Division: 1st Cav in Vietnam* (Novato, CA, 1987)

Tang, Truong Nhu, *A Vietcong Memoir* (New York, 1985)

Victory in Vietnam: The Official History of the People's Army of Vietnam, 1954–1975, trans. Merle Pribbenow (Lawrence, KS, 2002)

Villard, Eric B., *Staying the Course, October 1967 to September 1968* (Washington DC, 2017)

Warr, Nicholas, *Phase Line Green: The Battle for Hue, 1968* (Annapolis, MD, 1997)

Wiest, Andrew, *Vietnam's Forgotten Army: Heroism and Betrayal in the ARVN* (New York, 2007)

Willbanks, James H., *The Tet Offensive: A Concise History* (New York, 2006)

Wirtz, James J., *The Tet Offensive: Intelligence Failure in War* (Ithaca, NY, 1991)

INDEX